The COMPANIONS *in Christ* Network

www.companionsinchrist.org

So much more!

Companions in Christ is *so much more* than printed resources.
It offers an ongoing LEADERSHIP NETWORK that provides:

➤ Opportunities to connect with other small groups who are also journeying through the *Companions in Christ* series.

➤ Insights and testimonies from other *Companions in Christ* participants

➤ An online discussion room where you can share or gather information

➤ Training opportunities that develop and deepen the leadership skills used in formational groups

➤ Helpful leadership tips and articles as well as updated lists of supplemental resources

Just complete this form and drop it in the mail, and you can enjoy the many benefits available through the *Companions in Christ* NETWORK! Or, enter your contact information at www.companionsinchrist.org/leaders.

Name: *GEORGE KLINGMAN*

Address:

City/State/Zip:

Church:

Email:

Phone:

COMPANIONS *in Christ*
Upper Room Ministries
PO Box 340012
Nashville, TN 37203-9540

COMPANIONS *in Christ*
A SMALL-GROUP EXPERIENCE IN SPIRITUAL FORMATION

DEEPENING
~OUR PRAYER

Participant's Book   Volume 3

Adele J. Gonzales

UPPER ROOM BOOKS®
NASHVILLE

COMPANIONS IN CHRIST

DEEPENING OUR PRAYER: THE HEART OF CHRIST

Participant's Book: Part 3
Copyright © 2006 by Upper Room Books®
All rights reserved.

The Upper Room® Web site http://www.upperroom.org

UPPER ROOM®, UPPER ROOM BOOKS® and design logos are trademarks owned by the Upper Room®, a ministry of the GBOD®, Nashville, Tennessee. All rights reserved.

At the time of publication all Web sites referenced in this book were valid. However, due to the fluid nature of the Internet some addresses may have changed or the content may no longer be relevant.

Unless otherwise stated, scripture quotations are from the New Revised Standard Version Bible, copyright © 1989 by the Division of Christian Education of the National Council of the Churches of Christ in the U.S.A. Used by permission. All rights reserved.

Scripture quotations designated REB are from *The Revised English Bible* (a revision of The New English Bible) and © Oxford University Press and Cambridge University Press 1989. Reprinted with permission.

Scripture quotations designated KJV are from The King James Version of the Bible.

Cover design: Left Coast Design, Portland, OR
Cover photo: Richard Nowitz; National Geographic Photography/Getty Images
Interior icon development: Michael C. McGuire, settingPace
Second printing: 2008

LIBRARY OF CONGRESS CATALOGING-IN-PUBLICATION DATA

Gonzalez, Adele.
   Companions in Christ. Part 3, Deepening our prayer: the heart of Christ / Adele Gonzalez.
      p. cm.
   Includes bibliographical references and index.
   ISBN 978-0-8358-9832-4 (alk. paper)
  1. Prayer—Christianity. I. Title.

BV210.3.G66 2006
248.3'2—dc22

2005034886

Printed in the United States of America

For more information on *Companions in Christ*
call 800-972-0433 or visit www.companionsinchrist.org

Contents

Acknowledgments

Companions in Christ is truly the result of the efforts of a team of persons who shared a common vision. This team graciously contributed their knowledge and experience to develop a small-group resource that would creatively engage persons in a journey of spiritual growth and discovery. The author of Part 3 was Adele Gonzalez. Stephen Bryant was the primary author of the daily exercises and the Leader's Guide. Marjorie Thompson created the original design and participated in the editing of the entire resource. Keith Beasley-Topliffe served as a consultant in the creation of the process for the small-group meetings and contributed numerous ideas that influenced the final shape of the resource. In the early stages of development, two advisory groups read and responded to the initial drafts of material. The persons participating as members of those advisory groups were Jeannette Bakke, Avery Brooke, Thomas Parker, Helen Pearson Smith, Luther E. Smith Jr., Eradio Valverde Jr., Diane Luton Blum, Carol Bumbalough, Ruth Torri, and Mark Wilson. Prior to publication, test groups in the following churches used the material and provided helpful suggestions for improvement of the Participant's Books and the Leader's Guide.

First United Methodist Church, Hartselle, Alabama
St. George's Episcopal Church, Nashville, Tennessee

Acknowledgments

Northwest Presbyterian Church, Atlanta, Georgia
Garfield Memorial United Methodist Church,
　　Pepper Pike, Ohio
First United Methodist Church, Corpus Christi, Texas
Malibu United Methodist Church, Malibu, California
First United Methodist Church, Santa Monica, California
St. Paul United Methodist Church, San Antonio, Texas
Trinity Presbyterian Church, Arvada, Colorado
First United Methodist Church, Franklin, Tennessee
La Trinidad United Methodist Church, San Antonio, Texas
Aldersgate United Methodist Church, Slidell, Louisiana

My deep gratitude goes to all these persons and groups for their contribution to and support of *Companions in Christ*.

—Janice T. Grana, editor of *Companions in Christ*
April 2001

Introduction

*W*elcome to Part 3 of *Companions in Christ*, a small-group resource for spiritual formation designed to create a setting where you can respond to God's call to an ever-deepening communion and wholeness in Christ—as an individual, as a member of a small group, and as part of a congregation. The resource focuses on your experience of God and your discovery of spiritual practices that help you share more fully in the life of Christ. You will be exploring the potential of Christian community as an environment of grace and mutual guidance through the Spirit. You will grow closer to members of your small group as you seek together to know and respond to God's will. And your congregation will grow when you and your companions begin to bring what you learn into all areas of church life, from classes and meetings to worship and outreach.

How does *Companions in Christ* help you grow spiritually? It enables you to immerse yourself in "streams of living waters" through the spiritual disciplines of prayer, scripture, ministry, worship, study, and Christian conversation. These means of grace are the common ways in which Christ meets people, renews their faith, and deepens their life together in love. In the first part of *Companions in Christ* you were introduced to the concept of spiritual formation as a journey. In the second part you explored the depth of scripture. In this third part of *Companions in Christ*, you will experience new dimensions of prayer, try fresh ways of opening to God, and learn what it means to practice the presence of God. In the remaining units:

- You will reflect on Christ's call in your life and discover anew the gifts that God is giving you for living out your personal ministry.

- You and members of your group will grow together as a Christian community and gain skills in learning how small groups in the church become settings for spiritual guidance.

Although *Companions* is not an introductory course in Christianity for new Christians, it will help church people take up the basic disciplines of faith in renewing and transforming ways.

An Outline of the Resource

Companions in Christ has two primary components: individual reading and daily exercises throughout the week with this Participant's Book and a weekly two-hour meeting based on suggestions in the Leader's Guide. For each week, the Participant's Book has a chapter introducing new material and five daily exercises to help you reflect on your life in light of the content of the chapter. After the Preparatory Meeting of your group, you will begin a weekly cycle as follows: On day 1 you will be asked to read the chapter and on days 2–6 to complete the five daily exercises (found at the end of the chapter reading). On day 7 you will meet with your group. The daily exercises aim to help you move from information (knowledge about) to experience (knowledge of). An important part of this process is keeping a personal notebook or journal where you record reflections, prayers, and questions for later review and for reference at the weekly group meeting. The time commitment for the daily exercises is about thirty minutes. The weekly meeting will include time for reflecting on the exercises of the past week, for moving deeper into learnings from chapter readings, for having group experiences of prayer, and for considering ways to share with the congregation what you have learned or experienced.

The complete material in *Companions in Christ* covers a period of twenty-eight weeks divided into five parts or units, of which this volume is the third. The five parts are as follows:

1. *Embracing the Journey: The Way of Christ* (five weeks)—a basic exploration of spiritual formation as a journey toward wholeness and holiness, individually and in community, through the grace of God.

2. *Feeding on the Word: The Mind of Christ* (five weeks)—an introduction to several ways of meditating on and praying with scripture.

3. *Deepening Our Prayer: The Heart of Christ* (six weeks)—a guided experience of various forms and styles of prayer.

4. *Responding to Our Call: The Work of Christ* (five weeks)—a presentation of vocation or call: giving ourselves to God in willing obedience and receiving the fruits and gifts of the Holy Spirit.

5. *Exploring Spiritual Guidance: The Spirit of Christ* (five weeks)— an overview of different ways of giving and receiving spiritual guidance, from one-on-one relationships, to spiritual growth groups, to guidance in congregational life as a whole.

Your group may want to take a short break between units either to allow for some unstructured reflection time or to avoid meeting near Christmas or Easter. However, the units are designed to be sequential—each unit builds on previous ones.

This Participant's Book includes a section titled "Materials for Group Meetings." This section includes some brief supplemental readings that you will use as a part of one or more group meetings. Your leader will alert you when you will be using this material. Also you will find an annotated resource list that describes additional books related to the theme of this part of *Companions in Christ*.

You will need to bring your Participant's Book, your Bible, and your personal notebook or journal to the weekly group meeting.

The Companions in Christ Network

An additional dimension of *Companions in Christ* is the Network. While you and your group are experiencing *Companions in Christ*, groups in other congregations will also be meeting. The Network provides opportunities for you to share your experiences with one another and to link in a variety of meaningful ways. As you move through the resource, there will be occasions when you will be invited to pray for another group, send greetings or encouragement, or receive their support for your group. Connecting in these ways will enrich your group's experience and the experience of those to whom you reach out.

The Network also provides a place to share conversation and information. The Companion's Web site, www.companionsinchrist.org, includes a discussion room where you can offer insights, voice questions, and respond to others in an ongoing process of shared learning. The site provides a list of other Companions groups and their geographical locations so that you can make connections as you feel led.

The Companions Network is a versatile and dynamic component of the larger *Companions* resource. A Network toll-free number (1-800-972-0433) is staffed during regular business hours to take your order.

Your Personal Notebook or Journal

"I began these pages for myself, in order to think out my own particular pattern of living. . . . And since I think best with a pencil in my hand, I started naturally to write." Anne Morrow Lindbergh began her beloved classic, *Gift from the Sea*, with these words. You may not imagine that you "think best with a pencil in hand," but there is something truly wonderful about what can happen when we reflect on the inner life through writing.

Keeping a journal or personal notebook (commonly called journaling) will be one of the most important dimensions of your personal experience with *Companions in Christ*. The Participant's Book gives you daily spiritual exercises every week. More often than not, you will be asked to note your thoughts, reflections, questions, feelings, or prayers in relation to the exercises.

Even if you are totally inexperienced in this kind of personal writing, you may find that it becomes second nature very quickly. Your thoughts may start to pour out of you, giving expression to an inner life that has never been released. If, on the other hand, you find the writing difficult or cumbersome, give yourself permission to try it in a new way. Because a journal is "for your eyes only," you may choose any style that suits you. You need not worry about making your words sound beautiful or about writing with good grammar and spelling. You don't even need to write complete sentences! Jotting down key ideas, insights, or musings is just fine. You might want to doodle while you think or sketch an image that comes to you. Make journaling fun and relaxed. No one will see what you write, and you have complete freedom to share with the group only what you choose of your reflections.

There are two important reasons for keeping a journal or personal notebook as you move through *Companions in Christ*. First, the process of writing down our thoughts clarifies them for us. They become more specific and concrete. Sometimes we really do not know what we think until we see our thoughts on paper, and often the process of writing itself generates new creative insight. Second, this personal record captures what we have been experiencing inwardly over time. Journaling helps us track changes in our thinking and growth of insight. Our memories are notoriously fragile and fleeting in this regard. Specific feelings or creative connections we may have had two weeks ago, or even three days ago, are hard to recall without a written record. Even though your journal cannot capture all that goes through your mind in a single reflection period, it will serve as a reminder. You will need to draw on these reminders during small-group meetings each week.

Begin by purchasing a book that you can use for this purpose. It can be as simple as a spiral-bound notebook or as fancy as a cloth-bound blank book. Some people prefer lined paper and some unlined. You will want, at minimum, something more permanent than a ring-binder or paper pad. The Upper Room has made available a companion journal for this resource that you can purchase if you so desire.

When you begin the daily exercises, have your journal and pen or pencil at hand. You need not wait until you have finished reading and thinking an exercise through completely. Learn to stop and write as you go. Think on paper. Feel free to write anything that comes to you, even if it seems to be "off the topic." It may turn out to be more relevant or useful than you first think. If the process seems clumsy at first, don't fret. Like any spiritual practice, it gets easier over time, and its value becomes more apparent.

Here is how your weekly practice of journaling is shaped. On the first day after your group meeting, read the new chapter. Jot down your responses to the reading: "aha" moments, questions, points of disagreement, images, or any other reflections you wish to record. You may prefer to note these in the margins of the chapter. Over the next five days, you will do the exercises for the week, recording either general or specific responses as they are invited. On the day of the group meeting, it will be helpful to review what you have written through the week, perhaps marking portions you would like to share in the group. Bring your journal with you to meetings so that you can refer to it directly or refresh your memory of significant moments you want to paraphrase during discussion times. With time, you may indeed find that journaling helps you to think out your own pattern of living and that you will be able to see more clearly how God is at work in your life.

Your Group Meeting

The weekly group meeting is divided into four segments. First you will gather for a brief time of worship and prayer. This offers an opportunity to set aside the many concerns of the day and center on God's presence and guidance as you begin your group session.

The second section of the meeting is called "Sharing Insights." During this time you will be invited to talk about your experiences with the daily exercises. The group leader will participate as a member and share his or her responses as well. Generally the sharing by each member will be brief and related to specific exercises. This is an

important time for your group to learn and practice what it means
to be a community of persons seeking to listen to God and to live
more faithfully as disciples of Christ. The group provides a support-
ive space to explore your listening, your spiritual practices, and how
you are attempting to put those practices into daily life. Group members need not comment or offer advice to one another. Rather the
group members help you, by their attentiveness and prayer, to pay
attention to what has been happening in your particular response to
the daily exercises. The group is not functioning as a traditional support group that offers suggestions or help to one another. Rather, the
group members trust that the Holy Spirit is the guide and that they
are called to help one another listen to that guidance.

The "Sharing Insights" time presents a unique opportunity to
learn how God works differently in each of our lives. Our journeys,
while varied, are enriched by others' experiences. We can hold one
another in prayer, and we can honor each other's experience. Through
this part of the meeting, you will see in fresh ways how God's activity may touch or address our lives in unexpected ways. The group
will need to establish some ground rules to facilitate the sharing. For
example, you may want to be clear that each person speak only about
his or her own beliefs, feelings, and responses and that all group members have permission to share only what and when they are ready to
share. Above all, the group needs to maintain confidentiality so that
what is shared in the group stays in the group. This part of the group
meeting will be much less meaningful if persons interrupt and try to
comment on what is being said or try to "fix" what they see as a problem. The leader will close this part of the meeting by calling attention to any patterns or themes that seem to emerge from the group's
sharing. These patterns may point to a word that God is offering to the
group. Notice that the group leader functions both as a participant
and as someone who aids the process by listening and summarizing
the key insights that have surfaced.

The third segment of the group meeting is called "Deeper Explo-
rations." This part of the meeting may expand on ideas contained in

the week's chapter, offer practice in the spiritual disciplines introduced in the chapter or exercises, or give group members a chance to reflect on the implications of what they are learning for themselves and for their church. It offers a common learning experience for the group and a chance to go deeper in our understanding of how we can share more fully in the mind, heart, and work of Jesus Christ.

As it began, the group meeting ends with a brief time of worship, an ideal time for the group to share special requests for intercession that might come from the conversation and experience of the meeting or other prayer requests that arise naturally from the group.

The weeks that you participate in *Companions in Christ* will offer you the opportunity to focus on your relationship with Christ and to grow in your openness to God's presence and guidance. The unique aspect of this experience is that members of your small group, who are indeed your companions on the journey, will encourage your searching and learning. Those of us who have written and edited this resource offer our prayers that God will speak to you during these weeks and awaken you to enlarged possibilities of love and service in Christ's name. As we listen and explore together, we will surely meet our loving God who waits eagerly to guide us toward deeper maturity in Christ by the gracious working of the Holy Spirit.

Part 3

Deepening Our Prayer: The Heart of Christ

Adele J. Gonzalez

Prayer and the Character of God

Has anyone ever asked you about your prayer life? If so, how did the question make you feel? What did you answer? Over the years I have discovered how difficult it is for most Christians to talk or even think about their prayer life. Some of this hesitation may come from the cultural assumption that prayer is a private matter. It may also be that we feel inadequate to comprehend our prayer life or speak clearly about it. Whatever the reason, it appears that prayer, one of the foundational elements of our faith, remains unclear or uncomfortable for many Christians. This week we will look at some of our basic beliefs and assumptions about prayer.

The English word *prayer* comes from the Latin verb *precari*, which means "to entreat or beg." This definition indicates that we always stand in need before God, even when petition is not our intent. In prayer we do not speak *about* God; we speak *with* God. We choose to become present to God who is always present to us and to respond to the One who continually seeks to communicate with us. Prayer is offering God hospitality and opening ourselves to a deepening, personal relationship. In prayer we communicate with God verbally or silently, and we allow time and space for God to communicate with us. To pray is to surrender ourselves to God and to open our hearts, understanding, and wills to God.

The God to Whom We Pray

Without a clear conception of what God is like, where God is to be found, and how God relates to the world, we are likely to be hesitant and limited in prayer. So the starting place for a discussion of thinking about prayer can very reasonably be some reflection on how we can think about God.

—Martha Graybeal
Rowlett

In order to understand better the nature of Christian prayer, we need to understand something of the One to whom we pray. Who is God? What we believe about God shapes our prayer profoundly. Christian theology affirms that God is awesome in majesty, splendor, and power. The whole vast and intricate order of creation testifies to this. Indeed, the portrait we receive from the biblical record shows us God as the supreme source of all life whose power to create and recreate is complete. "For nothing will be impossible with God" (Luke 1:37). Yet God is also wise, just, and above all, loving. Therefore, God's power is exercised only in relation to love, "for God is love" (1 John 4:8). So God chooses to use power in a way that is completely consistent with the nature of divine love. Only such love can enable us to say without reserve, "God is good." Divine love frees us to approach the awesome power of God without being overcome by fear.

God's wisdom is an expression both of power and love. Wisdom includes justice and righteousness along with lovingkindness and compassion. God's wisdom is a source of deep consolation to us. Although we cannot understand its depths, we can trust that God knows what is best. God's understanding encompasses infinitely more than we can see, allowing God to act for the good of many persons simultaneously and even for the whole of creation.

A unique affirmation for Christians is that God is Trinitarian. That is, God is known in three persons: Father, Son, and Holy Spirit. The beginning of this doctrine lies in belief in the Incarnation. We believe that in Christ, the ineffable God has been revealed. Christ is the visible "image of the invisible God" (Col. 1:15), and "in him all the fullness of God was pleased to dwell" (Col. 1:19). Jesus Christ reveals to us a God who is essentially relational, who breaks through history, who loves passionately, and who empties God's self (Phil. 2:1-11). The Holy Spirit reveals and confirms these truths in our hearts (1 Cor. 2:6-16). By the Spirit we come to believe that Christ is the power and wisdom of God (1 Cor. 1:24) and the very love of God with us "in the flesh" (John 1:14; 3:16).

The three persons of the Trinity are united in a communion of perfect, mutual love. As persons made in the image of the Trinitarian God, we are created to be in communion with God and with one another. Prayer, in this context, is entering into the communion to which God calls us, a natural response of the heart to the One for whom we were made. Such prayer is definitely personal, but never private. Communion gathers us all into the heart of God.

These understandings of God's nature affect our perception of the act of prayer and how we enter into it. However, our personal histories and ideas also shape how we see and relate to God. Christians through the centuries have learned that as we discover more of God in prayer, we also find more of our true selves. What we are before God *is* what we are and nothing more. Prayer brings forth humility and truthfulness, revealing both our giftedness and our limitations. True prayer is always honest and authentic.

As prayer clarifies our self-understanding, we often discover discrepancies between the reality of God and our images of God. Our ideas about God affect deeply the ways we choose to communicate with God. Who is God for me? Do I see God as parent, judge, friend, or lover? What memories are connected to my images? If I perceive God as friend, I will probably desire to spend quality time in prayer. If I see God as unrelenting judge, I will probably avoid spending much time alone in God's company.

Some years ago, a friend of mine lost her three-year-old daughter to cancer. A well-meaning friend encouraged her to take heart because now "her little girl was in a better place." The friend explained that God had needed "a little angel in heaven" and had chosen her daughter. The grieving mother instantly rejected this "god" who did not seem to care about human suffering and loss. Any God who could take away her child in order to have another angel in heaven resembled more the thief who "comes to steal and kill and destroy" rather than the shepherd who has come "that they may have life, and have it abundantly" (John 10:10). For years, this woman searched for God in a variety of religions. Today she seems to have found some peace in praying to Mary, the mother of Jesus, as the only one able

If we are to grow up into Christ, we must be willing to push out the boundaries and accept the possibility of change—not change in the immutable God who was and is, but change in our perception and understanding of who this God is and who we are in relationship to God.

—Margaret Guenther

*O Lord, I have been
talking to the people;
Thought's wheels have
round me whirled a
fiery zone,
And the recoil of my
words' airy ripple
My heart unheedful
has puffed up and
blown.
Therefore I cast myself
before thee prone:
Lay cool hands on my
burning brain, and
press
From my weak heart
the swelling emptiness.*

—George MacDonald

to understand a mother's grief. In this specific case, the inadequate and false image of God as "thief" became an obstacle to her relationship with the living God.

During a faith-sharing meeting, a young man declared how tired he was of "chasing God," of trying so hard to reach God. A group member asked him who he thought God was. The man replied that as he grew up, God was always a judge, authoritative and remote. He went on to claim that his image had since changed to that of a merciful, loving God. Another group member suggested that perhaps he was trying too hard and that God still somewhat intimidated him. The man responded that he had not tried hard enough, that everyone knew how essential religious practices and disciplines were to attain a relationship with God. This man's early image of God was so deeply ingrained in him that he did not see how it continued to limit his perception of God's desire to be in communion with him. Oftentimes our images of God need to be healed before we can open ourselves to a life-giving prayer relationship.

Classic Postures of Prayer

If our images of God are rooted in grace and truth, we will pray out of our trust in God's goodness and faithfulness. We will open our hearts to this relationship because we believe ourselves to be beloved and wish to respond to this love in prayer.

As a relationship, prayer is dynamic and takes various expressions. The classic postures of prayer in the Christian tradition are adoration and praise, confession or contrition, thanksgiving, and supplication (petition and intercession). John Cassian, one of the early fathers of the church, wrote several treatises on the way prayer was organized in the monasteries at the end of the fourth and beginning of the fifth centuries. He explained, "There are as many types of prayer as there are different persons praying, nay as many as there are different states of mind" (*Collationes* 9.8). Cassian tried to present in an ascending order the kinds of prayers that Paul mentions briefly in 1 Timothy 2:1 (supplication, prayers of commitment, intercession, and thanksgiving).

Whether we consider these postures of prayer in ascending order, or simply as different expressions of our relationship with God, the important point to remember is that all these postures are interconnected and that each prayer contains some expression of the four. In prayer we acknowledge our neediness and our limitations. We are born helpless. As infants we cried when we were hungry or uncomfortable; we depended on others to meet our needs. As adults, particularly in our culture, we strive to become independent and self-sufficient. Sometimes this attitude impedes our awareness that before God we are always in need. Acknowledging our neediness does not mean a posture of slavery or dysfunctionality, but prayer reveals the truth of the creature before the Creator. It is an act of faith as we acknowledge that creation belongs to God and that God's creative presence is in everything. When we confess our limitations or ask for help, we reflect our grateful trust in a God who cares for us and who wishes to hear the deepest desires of our hearts. Thus, petition and confession contain elements of adoration and thanksgiving. As we discover God's presence in our lives, we joyfully adore the divine mystery and grandeur and at the same time thank God for the liberating action of Jesus Christ in human history.

To Pray as Jesus Did

As we consider the importance of prayer in the Christian life, the example of Jesus' own prayer life and his teachings concerning prayer are instructive. For Jesus, prayer was always an encounter with Abba, Father, a name of extraordinary intimacy in Hebrew. In this communion, Jesus gradually learned more fully the meaning of his own identity and God's plan of salvation. In the Gospels we see the centrality of prayer to Jesus' way of life from beginning to end. Jesus prayed at the beginning of his public ministry when he was baptized by John (Luke 3:21-22), and it was in prayer at the end of his earthly life that Jesus fully yielded his will to the Father's will (Luke 22:41-42). At important moments in his life, Jesus devoted special time to prayer. For example, he spent the night in prayer before choosing his

twelve disciples (Luke 6:12), and he went to a deserted place to pray after a long day of healing ministry (Luke 4:42). He prayed a prayer of gratitude and praise when the disciples returned from one of their missionary journeys (Matt. 11:25-26). While praying he was transfigured before Peter, James, and John (Luke 9:28-29). Jesus turned to God in his moment of profound pain and loneliness (Mark 15:34) on the cross, and finally, with his last breath, surrendered everything to God (Luke 23:46).

Jesus taught the necessity of prayer when confronting evil (Mark 9:29), and he taught about the power of uniting with others in prayer (Matt. 18:19-20). Jesus always asked for honesty in prayer. He called all who would listen to pray sincerely from the heart and to validate their prayer in action (Matt. 7:21-23; 15:8-9; Mark 12:40; Luke 18:11-13). Our Lord encouraged his followers to pray with confidence (Matt. 21:21-22). Just as prayer was at the core of Jesus' life and ministry, so it is for us as his followers. Our prayer should be marked by the same qualities as his: trust in God, intimacy, sincerity, honesty, integrity, and gratitude.

Prayer and Commitment

Jesus' prayer in Gethsemane reveals to us most clearly his willingness to trust utterly in God's goodness and higher wisdom. On that night, before his arrest, Jesus was distressed and agitated, experiencing deep grief (Mark 14:34). Jesus has begun his public life with God's profound baptismal affirmation "You are my Son, the Beloved; with you I am well pleased" (Mark 1:11). Now his sonship will be tested to the full. Gethsemane shows us a time of intense inward struggle in Jesus' heart and soul. The messianic task seems too painful to endure. In this final hour, Jesus, in an agony of spirit, prays once again: "Abba, Father, for you all things are possible; remove this cup from me" (Mark 14:36). Then his surrender and commitment to God prevail: "Not what I want, but what you want" (Mark 14:36).

The Gospel of Mark, the shortest and the earliest of the four Gospels, presents a hurried, human Jesus. It has been said of this

Growth in the life of faith demands a constant willingness to let go and leap again. Prayer is not always a smooth, peaceful progress, but a series of detachments from everything . . . that is not God.

—Maria Boulding

Gospel that if Jesus ever sat down, Mark failed to record it! The Gospel writer presents Jesus' grief and acceptance of God's will in a single verse, giving the impression that it took only seconds for Jesus to move from intense suffering to total abandonment to God. Regardless of the length of the struggle, the depth and vitality of Jesus' prayer enabled him at this critical moment to hold fast to his vocation and remain faithful to God even unto death (Phil. 2:8; Heb. 5:7-10). Jesus had a stronger commitment to God's reign than to his own life.

Similarly, when we pray, we make an implicit commitment to the vision of God's reign offered by Jesus and express our decision to follow in his footsteps. This is particularly evident in the prayer we commonly call the Lord's Prayer. Luke tells us that one day when Jesus was praying in a certain place, one of the disciples said to him, "Lord, teach us to pray." Jesus' response is the heart of Christian prayer:

Father, hallowed be your name.	*Adoration*
Your kingdom come.	*Surrender*
Give us each day our daily bread.	*Supplication*
And forgive us our sins,	*Confession*
for we ourselves forgive everyone	
indebted to us.	*Commitment to Follow*
And do not bring us to the time of trial.	*Supplication*
(Luke 11:1-4)	

We can pray such a prayer with a grateful heart when we truly believe that "neither death, nor life, nor angels, nor rulers, nor things present, nor things to come, nor powers, nor height, nor depth, nor anything else in all creation, will be able to separate us from the love of God in Christ Jesus our Lord" (Rom. 8:38-39). Only as we grow into a deep assurance of God's faithful love and care for us can we commit ourselves without reserve to the reign of God.

Our relationship with God is multifaceted. At times, it is like a parent-child relationship. Sometimes it has the character of a master-servant relationship; at others, it is like the relationship between friends. It may even resemble the intimacy between lovers. As we mature in faith, we tend to grow from the child or servant relationship into the friend or lover relationship. Jesus tells his disciples at the end of three years together that he no longer calls them servants but friends because he has shared with them his own intimate knowledge of God (John 15:15). The more we know God personally in the relationship of prayer, the more that relationship becomes friendship between God, who is Love, and ourselves, God's beloved.

In prayer we are invited to respond to God's initiative with attentiveness, openness, humility, and honesty. As we grow into deeper intimacy with the divine Friend, our prayer becomes more trusting. We trust in God's presence even when we cannot perceive or feel it, even when we cannot pray or do not know how to pray. We are confident in God's steadfast love in our pain and in our joy. We come to see that our God asks us not for perfect prayers, whatever we may imagine them to be, but for fidelity to the relationship that God, the lover of our souls, so deeply desires. The ultimate goal of the Christian life is union with God through Christ. It is a union of wills, in love, expressed symbolically and beautifully in the poem known as the Song of Solomon.

> I am my beloved's,
>   and his desire is for me.
> Come, my beloved,
>   let us go forth into the fields,
>   and lodge in the villages. . . .
> There I will give you my love (7:10-12).

To live the life of prayer means to emerge from my drowse, to awaken to the communing, guiding, healing, clarifying, and transforming current of God's Holy Spirit in which I am immersed.

—Douglas V. Steere

DAILY EXERCISES

Read the chapter for Week 1 titled "Prayer and the Character of God." Mark the parts that yield insight, challenge, or questions for you. In preparation, quiet yourself and reflect on the following words:

> Like the spiritual life itself, prayer is initiated by God. No matter what we think about the origin of our prayers, they are all a response to the hidden workings of the Spirit within.[1]

This week's daily exercises focus on the development of the practice of prayer in your life.

EXERCISE 1

Read 1 Samuel 3:1-14. This is a story about the boy Samuel and how Eli helps him recognize and respond to the voice of the Lord. What are your earliest experiences of prayer? What was your understanding of prayer as a child, and how has it changed? Who or what helped you recognize and respond to the presence of God in your life?

Devote at least five minutes of time to becoming present to God—the God who is with you now—and to focusing on God's love for you. Do so in whatever way helps you and seems authentic for you.

EXERCISE 2

Read Luke 11:1-4. One of Jesus' disciples asks him to teach them to pray. What do you feel this disciple really wanted? Put yourself in the his place and personalize the request to Jesus. What about you? What do you seek as you set out on this journey of "deepening your prayer"?

Devote at least five minutes of your time to becoming present to God—the God who is with you now. Do so in whatever way helps you and seems real. Take time to record your experience in your journal.

EXERCISE 3

Read Luke 11:1-4. Read the story with an eye and ear to the prayer Jesus taught his disciples to pray. On page 23, notice how the successive phrases of the Lord's Prayer invite you to assume several "postures" of prayer (adoration, surrender, etc.) in your relationship with God. Which phrase in the prayer represents your most common posture

before God? your least comfortable posture that challenges you to grow in your life with God?

Devote five minutes of your time to becoming present to God and responding to the fullness of God's call. Do so in whatever way you can. Take a moment to record your experience in your journal.

EXERCISE 4

Read Psalm 18:1-2, a psalm of adoration and praise to the Lord. Notice how in two verses the psalmist employs more than ten images to praise God and name who God is! Reflect on the adequacy of these images as expressions of your own praise and adoration for God. Personalize Psalm 18:1-2 by rewriting it and adding your own images for God.

Take five minutes to celebrate God's presence and express yourself to God in whatever way seems best (sitting, walking, dancing, singing). Record your experience in your journal.

EXERCISE 5

Read the following prayer (from Augustine's *Confessions*) slowly, out loud if possible. Let it penetrate your heart.

> I came to love you late, O Beauty, so ancient, so new.
> I came to love you late!
> Look! You were internal and I was external,
> running about in my ugly fashion,
>   seeking you in the beautiful things you made.
> You were with me, but I was not with you.
> Those things kept me far from you,
> even though if they were not in you, they would not be at all.
> You called and cried out and broke open my deafness.
> You gleamed and shone and chased away my blindness.
> I breathed in your fragrance and pant for more.
>   I tasted and now hunger and thirst.
>   You touched me and I burn for your presence.[2]

Devote five minutes to allowing Augustine's prayer to lead you into an awareness of God's presence. Take a moment to record your experience in your journal.

Review your week's journal entries to prepare for the group meeting.

Part 3, Week 2
Dealing with Impediments to Prayer

Recently, I heard a woman talk about her prayer life with some friends in a faith-sharing group. She was frustrated, and her friends wanted to help. At their prompting she explained that for the past few weeks her prayer had been "dry," and she was not getting anything out of it. Since I had been invited to participate that night in their group, I asked the woman to tell us more about what she called dryness. She told how she had always been able to express her needs to the Lord and to feel comforted in her prayer times. "The words just flowed," she said, "and it was always such a beautiful experience! I sensed the Lord's presence so deeply, and I always felt inspired and uplifted. But now, I don't feel anything anymore, and words just do not come to my mind. When they do, they seem to fall flat, as if they were hitting a ceiling or bouncing around in my head. I just don't feel connected anymore!" Other members of the group confessed that at times they had experienced the same problem in their prayer.

This situation is not uncommon. Many Christians think that prayer should always be easy, natural, and spontaneous. We want to express ourselves in meaningful ways and to experience a sense of God's presence as we pray. We feel a sense of accomplishment when we can tell God clearly all that is in our hearts and minds. And certainly we experience comfort and inspiration in the feelings that can accompany our prayers. Could we be placing too much importance

on what we say and feel, and not enough on what God wants to communicate to us?

Praying is not always easy, natural, or spontaneous. If we take our prayer life seriously, we will likely experience times when praying becomes a challenge and a struggle. Many things such as fatigue, fear, doubt, illness, changing perceptions, and strong emotions can come between us and our prayer. It helps to look at these and see what we can learn from them about ourselves and our relationship with God. This week we will look at some common misunderstandings about prayer. We will also reflect on what we experience as obstacles to prayer and how we can deal with them.

Misunderstandings of Prayer

The First Letter of John reminds us, "In this is love, not that we loved God but that he loved us" (4:10). As I have said, prayer is always our response to the God who loves us and desires to be in communion with us. A meaningful prayer life is not something we achieve by pointing to our own merits or by becoming "spiritual gymnasts" who master a variety of techniques. While spiritual practices and methods facilitate our disposition to prayer, prayer itself remains a response of the heart to the free initiative of our loving God.

Many people doubt God's unconditional love and availability. Sometimes our life experiences make this truth hard to believe. We tend to compare God with people and to imagine God in human ways. If my father was not there for me as a child when I needed him, then I may well have believed that God, the Father, could not possibly be there either. If our parents were stern, rigid disciplinarians, always ready to judge and criticize, we may have difficulty accepting the idea that God's love is unconditional or that "divine judgment" serves the larger purpose of redemption and restoration. If we become frustrated in our attempts to pray, we may imagine that God is also tired of trying to connect with us. Because human love has limits, we tend to place limits on God's infinite love. But prayer invites us to ponder the mystery of God's utterly faithful way of loving.

Prayer is communion with God. It is a matter of making connections with the One who stands at the center of all life and joy, and of learning to live with those connections all the time.

—John Killinger

In the book of the prophet Hosea we find a particularly encouraging passage. Using some of the most touching images in prophetic literature, Hosea compares Israel to a wife to whom the Lord says, "I will take you for my wife in faithfulness; and you shall know the Lord" (Hos. 2:20). The prophet also compares God's love with that of a parent: "When Israel was a child, I loved him. . . . / It was I who taught Ephraim to walk, / I took them up in my arms. . . . / I led them with cords of human kindness, / with bands of love. / I was to them like those who lift infants to their cheeks" (Hos. 11:1, 3-4). But God also laments deeply the people's turning away and worshiping other gods. God struggles with a desire to give up on Israel in "fierce anger" (Hos. 11:9). In a beautiful soliloquy that has been preserved as a gem of the prophetic tradition, the Lord exclaims, "I will not again destroy Ephraim; for I am God and no mortal" (Hos. 11:9). This is the core truth that we find difficult to comprehend. God is not like us! When we enter prayer, we need not fear that God is too tired or irritated to be present to us. God is no mortal. God is faithful!

Because of this faithfulness, we can trust that in prayer we always meet God, whether our experience of prayer is easy or difficult. We can also trust that God's love and desire for us are greater than our ability to utter "good prayers" or even deeply felt prayers. We enter prayer as a response to God who already possesses us by love, not in an effort to reach One who is trying to elude us. For Christians, prayer is a sure encounter with God but not necessarily in the way we expect or desire. In our efforts to "succeed" with our personal agendas, we may fail to receive the unconditional love and intimacy that God freely offers in unexpected ways.

Christian prayer is always contextual; that is, it is affected by who we are, what we do, where we live, and how we feel. We are finite in the ways we respond to God. Often we experience certain elements of life as impediments to prayer. We are too tired, do not have enough time, do not have sufficient space in our crowded houses, or do not feel the way we think we should. Prayer can prompt one of the most poignant struggles of the Christian life and yet without a vital prayer life, genuine growth in faith is impeded.

Provided that we don't give up, the Lord will guide everything for our benefit, even though we may not find someone to teach us. There is no other remedy for this evil of giving up prayer than to begin again; otherwise the soul will gradually lose more each day.

—Teresa of Avila

Among the variety of obstacles to prayer, I have chosen to address three that surface most frequently in my life and ministry.

Time as an Obstacle

The first impediment is often expressed this way: "I don't have enough time! Between my job, family, and other commitments, twenty-four hours are never enough!" We live in a complicated, busy society, and our cares are many. Yet I am amazed at the many things we squeeze into our busy schedules when they seem important enough.

I remember one morning when I had decided I did not have time to pray. As I was preparing to leave for work, the doorbell rang. A service man from a local store was there to fix a recently installed appliance. He apologized for showing up unannounced but explained that he was in the neighborhood and had taken the opportunity to pay a call to my house. I welcomed him warmly and thanked him for thinking of us. Promptly, I called my office to say that I was going to be an hour or so late. I knew this would further cramp my day but could not pass up the opportunity to have my kitchen appliance serviced. Later, as I was driving to the office, a question popped into my head: Where did that hour come from? The bottom line was that I needed the repair and my decision was cost-effective! I was not sure I would have felt better if I had devoted the same hour to prayer on that hectic morning. With the repair man I got the results I wanted; maybe with God I would not have gotten my way.

Sometimes the time factor serves as an excuse to mask feelings of apathy or anxiety in prayer. While our feelings are important and God uses them to communicate with us, we must not allow them to determine our fidelity to the relationship. We pray not to "feel good" but to be faithful.

While few of us have much spare time, we often do not take advantage of time we have. Take, for example, the waiting room in a doctor's office. We check our watches frequently, hoping that time will move faster. We may read magazines, watch a little television, or observe people. Why not use these precious minutes or hours to connect intentionally with God? Last week a friend told me that her entire attitude about driving had changed dramatically when she started to pray in the car (not with her eyes closed!). She recounted how, when detained in heavy traffic, she used to become very frustrated and even violent. Now she thanks God for this slow time alone and feels that for the first time she is heeding Paul's advice to "pray without ceasing" (1 Thess. 5:17).

Giving time to prayer is a matter of priority and intention. We will make time for the relationship prayer expresses, if truly desired. Moreover, with hearts tuned in to God's presence in the midst of life, we will discover hidden calls to prayer in the daily round of activities.

Need for Control

A second key obstacle to a deeper, truer life of prayer is our need to control outcomes. In prayer we are called to let go, to surrender ourselves to God who loves us and knows us in ways we cannot even begin to imagine. Letting go is difficult, in part, because we do not trust that God's answers to our prayers, or even the experience of prayer itself, will be what we want them to be. As Christians, we sometimes claim that we trust completely in God's ways. Yet many of us try to tell God exactly what we want, as well as when and how we want it. When we pray, are we trusting in God or in our own intelligent opinions? I have heard people claim that we show great trust in God when we expect to get what we ask for. This is perhaps based on scripture passages reassuring us that "everyone who asks receives" (Matt. 7:8). However, many of us practice what I call selective listening to the Word of God. We fail to hear that whatever the specific hopes and desires of our prayers, God will give "good things to those who ask" (Matt. 7:11). Are we sure that in our prayer we are asking for these good things? God asks us to "strive first for the kingdom of God . . . and all these things will be given . . . as well" (Matt. 6:33). Is our prayer about seeking first the kingdom or about the things to be given us? In the Gospel of Luke, Jesus tells Martha that she is worried and distracted by many things (Luke 10:41). I wonder if our prayer is as honestly

We must in all our prayers carefully avoid wishing to confine God to certain circumstances, or prescribe to God the time, place, or mode of action. . . . For before we offer up any petition for ourselves, we ask that God's will may be done, and by so doing place our will in subordination to God's.

—John Calvin

trusting as Jesus': "Father . . . not what I want but what you want" (Matt. 26:39); "Our Father . . . your will be done, on earth as it is in heaven" (Matt. 6:10).

Mary questioned the angel who told of Jesus' birth; Joseph too had his doubts. Many times the disciples did not seem to understand when Jesus spoke of the kingdom of God. Yet, because of their yes, belief in Jesus is possible today. Is the attitude we take to prayer our own yes, a surrender to God's ways, trusting in God's mercy and love for us? Entering into prayer means taking a risk. We may not hear what we want to hear, or worse, we may not hear anything. A French spiritual writer of the seventeenth century, Jean-Pierre de Caussade, once wrote:

> The great and firm foundation of the spiritual life is the offering of ourselves to God and being subject to his will in all things. . . . Once we have this foundation, all we need to do is spend our lives rejoicing that God is God and being so wholly abandoned to his will that we are quite indifferent as to what we do and equally indifferent as to what use he makes of our activities. Our main duty is to abandon ourselves.[1]

Desiring to control the outcome of prayer may result from our fears and anxieties or lack of faith. An excessive need for control is founded either on secular values or on deep psychological needs rather than on the gospel message and the lifestyle of Christian disciples.

Fear of What We May Discover about Ourselves

A recent experience with a friend illustrates the final obstacle to prayer I want to address. A few weeks ago, this friend committed to spend one hour each day praying with scripture. When I saw her last week, she seemed eager to share her experience. After some initial hesitation, she confided that the past days had been very difficult for her. "Things that I thought were forgotten surfaced again," she exclaimed with dismay. As I listened, she continued, "There are areas in my life that I considered healed, but memories have come back to upset me. I don't like the way I am feeling. I was sure that I had left behind all anger and resentment, but they are still in me. I don't like myself when

I feel this way!" When I asked how she was dealing with her discomfort, she answered, "I don't think it was a good idea for me to pray so much at this time. Maybe I'll start this discipline again at a later time."

When we pray, we encounter not only God but also our own truth, the brokenness of our human condition. This is not a comfortable reality to face. It may help to remember Jesus' identification with everything that is deepest in our humanity, including strong emotions such as fear and anger. Jesus' prayers stand as evidence of his intimate relationship with God even as he confronted the challenges of his humanity. Christian prayer is neither therapy to obtain tranquility nor a relaxation technique. Encountering the living God sometimes shatters the surface peacefulness of our lives.

Prayer has been compared to a furnace of transformation. If we are willing to see clearly what is in our hearts and offer it to God, we gradually discover what it means to be conformed to the image of God. But staying open to the process is often painful and frustrating. If God seeks and loves us and we willingly respond, why all these difficulties? Again we turn to Jesus, God among us, taking on all aspects of our humanity, including our fatigue, frustration, and disappointment. His total surrender on the cross was not about understanding but about surrendering. We can bring our feelings of frustration, discomfort, and disappointment right into our prayer and wait in faith for God's response. We can express honestly our fears and discomfort and listen for the word God will speak to us. Alongside Jesus, we take prayer as a relationship between two friends, humbly accepting that the human condition limits one of the two. As we continue to journey in faithfulness, we join the blind men of the Gospel of Matthew: "Have mercy on us, Son of David!" (Matt. 9:27).

Begin where you are. Obey now. Use what little obedience you are capable of, even if it be like a grain of mustard seed. Begin where you are. Live this present moment, this present hour as you now sit in your seats, in utter, utter submission and openness toward [God].

—Thomas R. Kelly

DAILY EXERCISES

Read the chapter for Week 2, "Dealing with Impediments to Prayer."
Keep a journal or blank book beside you to record your thoughts,
questions, prayers, and images. Begin your exercises by thinking about
the following quotation:

> In learning to pray, no laboratory is needed but a room, no apparatus
> but ourselves. The living God is the field of force into which we enter
> in prayer, and the only really fatal failure is to stop praying and not to
> begin again.[2]

These exercises will challenge you to identify the impediments to
prayer in your life and to look carefully at your resistance to God's
presence in your life.

Exercise 1

Read Isaiah 44:6-11. What are the common idols of our day? Identify a popular image of God with which you struggle or which makes
prayer difficult for you (such as angry parent, distant creator, divine
accountant, legalistic judge, chief executive of the universe, male God).
Draw this image.

Now consider what image of God opens you to the divine presence and facilitates prayer (for example, shepherd, loving parent, creator, light)? Draw a symbol that expresses your truest image of God.

Devote several minutes to being present to God, who exceeds all
our images and yet becomes real to us in Christ, "the image of the
invisible God" (Col. 1:15). Record your experience in your journal.

Exercise 2

Read Matthew 26:36-46. In this passage, Jesus prays in the garden of
Gethsemane, and the disciples cannot stay awake with him for even
one hour. What do you think might have caused the disciples to have
trouble staying awake and available to Jesus? Reflect on the three
impediments to prayer described in this week's chapter. Which con-
tributes most to your difficulty staying awake spiritually? Record your
thoughts in your journal.

Devote at least five minutes to being present and available to Christ without falling asleep. Record your experience, insights, and challenges.

EXERCISE 3

Read Psalm 139:1-18. Explore how you feel about God's searching you and knowing you. Draw an image of your life as a house with rooms for each dimension of you (such as family, work, church, etc.). Invite the Lord to take an imaginary walk with you through the house. Notice your feelings about God and about yourself as you go from room to room. Also notice the Lord's response to each room. Reflect in your journal on how your feelings about your life or God may translate into either readiness or reluctance to pray.

Devote several minutes to opening afresh some part of your life to God's searching and knowing presence. Record your experience.

EXERCISE 4

Read Mark 9:2-9. In this story, Jesus leads his disciples "up a high mountain apart, by themselves" to experience him and themselves in God's transforming presence. Peter interrupts the experience with ideas about how to improve it, preserve it, or do something useful with it. What in you often interrupts your being present to God?

Devote at least ten minutes to being present to God, centering your attention on the voice that says, "This is my Son, the Beloved; listen to him!" Record your insights and experience.

EXERCISE 5

Read Matthew 11:28. Use your entire time to listen deeply to God. Leave your prayer time in God's hands. Do not work too hard. You might begin with Jesus' invitation: "Come to me, all you that are weary and are carrying heavy burdens, and I will give you rest." Rest in the Lord and release your heaviness to God. At the end of your time of silence, record your awareness, feelings, insights, surprises, or other responses in your journal.

Review your journal for the week in preparation for the group meeting.

Part 3, Week 3
Prayers of Petition and Intercession

Some time ago, my friend Sarah's father suffered a heart attack. Luckily Sarah was visiting him at the time. She administered CPR until the paramedics arrived and took him to a nearby hospital. After his condition improved, Sarah told a church group of her gratitude for the opportunity to have saved her father's life. She felt that God had guided her and protected her father. Many of her church friends gathered to offer prayers of thanksgiving for what Sarah considered her "little miracle." After a quick recovery, Sarah's father was released from the hospital and returned home to his family.

A few months later, Sarah called me. Her father had just been diagnosed with a malignant brain tumor. He was experiencing double vision and other symptoms. The tumor, the doctor said, was inoperable. His condition rapidly deteriorated. At the time of his death a few months later, he was unable to see, hear, or speak; he was a withered body lying on the bed, with no hope of recovery. My friend felt deeply anguished. Not only had her father died a painful and humiliating death, but she considered herself responsible for the catastrophe. "I should have let him die," she would cry. "At least he would have died in peace. Why did God allow this to happen?" I never found the right words to console her. I could only listen and hold her in prayer.

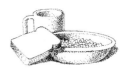

This story disturbs our deepest sensibilities, raising many natural and difficult questions. What happened here? Did God fail Sarah? Did Sarah "fail" her father by saving him in the first crisis? Did family and friends pray for the wrong thing?

Prayers of petition and intercession can be mystifying. Sometimes we feel that our prayers go unanswered, and we question the value of asking for anything at all. Other times, as in Sarah's case, we wonder if we have sought or asked for the wrong thing. If we cannot really know what is best for anyone at any given time, why ask at all? For centuries these questions have been the subject of debate and countless conversations in religious circles. Many books have been written on the topic, and Christians continue to wonder about them. We may not have clarity on all these issues, but we do know that Christ urges us to make our requests known to a God who loves us and cares for us. This week we will focus on prayers of petition and intercession, prayers for ourselves and prayers for others.

Prayer of Petition

In prayer we open ourselves to the chance that God will do something with us that we had not intended.

—Emilie Griffin

Petition means "to ask or to beseech." Petition is one of the fundamental stances of the human being before the mystery of God. Just as in adoration we recognize the wonder of God, in our prayers of petition we acknowledge our dependency on God. Because we believe in a relational God, we also believe that God desires a personal relationship with us. In this context we offer petitions for ourselves. Petition connects our human need with faith in a God who cares for us and desires our good. The problem arises when we think that we know what is best for ourselves and allow the conviction of our "knowing" to shape our petition. We earnestly pray for what we perceive to be the joy, healing, or goodness we need, forgetting that the prayer of petition is not a tool to manipulate God but a response to God out of our poverty and need. Humans cannot control the mystery of God's will. Yet often when we do not receive the desired answers to our requests, we feel resentful and hopeless.

I would like to suggest two necessary elements in our prayer of petition: (1) a willingness to ask, trusting the deep goodness and love in God's response, whether or not we can see it as such; and (2) a willingness to receive what comes as from the hand of God, surrendering to the divine will in an act of faith.

Asking. We present our needs to God, although God fully knows them already. "Even before a word is on my tongue, O Lord, you know it completely" (Ps. 139:4). The psalmist's awareness of God's omniscience does not prevent him from crying out to God: "You are my God; give ear, O Lord, to the voice of my supplications" (Ps. 140:6); "Incline your ear, O Lord, and answer me, for I am poor and needy" (Ps. 86:1). Like the psalmist, we do not pray to inform God of our needs; we pray because we depend on God and trust in God's love for us.

Often our prayers help us perceive our true needs more clearly. We may imagine that our need is for physical healing when the root need is for emotional or relational healing. We may begin by praying earnestly for a particular outcome and find over time that our prayers get "sifted" in God's presence. Self-centered, anxious, and superfluous aspects of our prayer simply fall away as the Spirit purifies our desires. This falling away is part of how God works to reshape our will so that it conforms more closely to God's perfect will. Jesus encourages us to seek, ask, and knock so that good gifts may be given by God and found by us (see Luke 11:9-10). More than anything, God wants to "give the Holy Spirit to those who ask him" (Luke 11:13). This is the greatest of gifts, the one that orders all else we could hope to seek because the Spirit discerns truly what is the will of God (see Rom. 8:27).

Petition, then, is not aimed at changing God's heart because God already desires the best for us. Instead, it unites our desires to those things that God already wishes to give us but that require our consent to be granted. Every time we ask God to come to our assistance, we open ourselves to the coming of God's kingdom within and among us. When we pray as Jesus taught us to pray, we ask for many things:

material sustenance, pardon, strength in our weakness, wisdom in our confusion, and comfort in our suffering. We come in faith to ask God, the giver of life, to sustain our spiritual, physical, and emotional life. We ask for the deep healing that may or may not include the cure of our illnesses. Above all, we ask for the grace of the Holy Spirit and the fulfillment of God's kingdom (Matt. 6:10).

Receiving. When we present our petitions to God, we yield to the one who knit us together in the womb (Ps. 139:13) and who knows us better than we know ourselves: "Before I formed you in the womb I knew you" (Jer. 1:5). My friend Sarah did not know what was best for her father. God is the only one who really knew. She thought it would have been better had he died "peacefully" of a heart attack. Others suggested that her father needed the extra time to prepare better for his final encounter with God. We can only guess what was in God's mind in this situation; but more important, we can trust what is in God's heart.

In prayers of petition and intercession, we exclaim with the psalmist, "I delight to do your will, O my God; your law is within my heart" (Ps. 40:8). Receptivity to God's response does not mean a resigned passivity to what God has already decided without our involvement. On the contrary, when we willingly yield ourselves to God, we become active collaborators in the divine plan, full-time participants in God's project for creation. By uniting our will to God's will, we join in Jesus' Gethsemane prayer. In fully accepting God's will, Jesus fulfilled his identity as God's Son, the Beloved, with whom God was well pleased (Luke 3:22). As we come to accept and desire God's will fully, we too fulfill the human identity we have been given as sons and daughters of the living God.

> To pray for others means to offer others a hospitable place where I can really listen to their needs and pains.
>
> —Henri J. M. Nouwen

Prayer of Intercession

Because we believe ourselves to be children of the one God, we express our solidarity and communion when we pray on behalf of others. In the Hebrew Scriptures we find great intercessors such as Abraham, Moses, and the prophets, who kept calling the people back to fidelity to the covenant and interceded for their sins. The Suffering Servant offers a biblical model of intercessory prayer: "He bore the sin of many, and made intercession for the transgressors" (Isa. 53:12). The author of the Letter to the Hebrews assigns this role to Jesus: Jesus as the great intercessor, the high priest, the mediator of the new covenant, offered once to bear the sins of many (Heb. 7:26; 9:15, 28). Paul offers Jesus' intercessory role as our hope in his Letter to the Romans, which presents Christ, not as the one who is to condemn, but as the one "who died, yes, who was raised, who is at the right hand of God, who indeed intercedes for us" (8:34). As Christians we maintain that God alone can grant us good things and that Christ is our true mediator or intercessor before God. When we offer prayers of intercession on behalf of others, we express our common need as children of the one God and join our intentions with the heart of Christ who purifies and presents our needs before God.

God is continually working out a redemptive process in this world, and God uses the faith of believing persons in the mysterious working of this process. Our prayers can and do make a difference. They are, as one writer puts it, "a cosmic fact, that . . . may tip the balance."[1] The tremendous dignity and privilege of being able to join God's saving, transforming intentions for this world should give us great courage in our prayers.

We do not have enough conviction about prayer. If we pray only a little, our prayers are answered only to that degree. If we pray much, we receive many answers. Christ's activity was founded on prayer. We must not make ourselves alone the center, but our prayers must show a sense of responsibility toward God . . . for the whole world.

—Toyohiko Kagawa

What to Pray For

Sarah and her friends questioned the legitimacy of their prayer. Like them, we really do not know what is best for anyone. What then do we pray for in our petitions and intercessions?

I have said that we pray because we trust God's promise to help us in our need. The question then is, "What do we really need?" In some situations, the need is most apparent, and we want to pray for those needs in a concrete fashion. Yet beyond the obvious needs, I would like to suggest three common human needs, necessary elements in our quest for healing, that we often overlook in our prayers of petition and intercession. They are our need for love, forgiveness, and peace.

Intercession is not only the best arbitrator of all differences, the best promoter of true friendship, the best cure and preservative against all unkind tempers, all angry and haughty passions, but is also of great use to discover to us the true state of our own hearts.

—William Law

When we stand before God, we realize how wounded we are, how sinful and limited our human response to God's love is. Like the tax collectors and sinners of Jesus' time, we come near to listen to him. Some would remind us that we do not deserve to be close to Jesus, that we are not good enough to enjoy his love. To those arguments Jesus responds with the parable of the prodigal son (Luke 15:11-32). Through this powerful story, Jesus reveals to us the unconditional love of a God who desires to welcome us back into the Father's house, not because of our deep contrition, but because of God's outrageous love. When we pray, we need to ask for openness to this love, to invite God's mercy into our lives. God's greatest desire is to be in communion with each one of us. This was Jesus' promise: "Those who love me will keep my word, and my Father will love them, and we will come to them and make our home with them" (John 14:23). Nothing could be more intimate. We need to ask for the grace to accept God's love for ourselves and for others, so that we in turn may love God and offer ourselves as the dwelling place of the eternal Lover!

We also need to ask for forgiveness for ourselves and for others, and for the grace to accept it. Many of us have difficulty letting go of the past. We cling to our guilt and our sin, even though God has already forgotten them. Recently I heard someone suggest that God throws our sins in a lake and then posts a "No Fishing" sign by it. To accept God's forgiveness and to forgive ourselves for being less than perfect are necessary conditions for our openness to forgive others. Our prayers of petition include asking for forgiveness and for the grace to extend that forgiveness to those who offend us.

Finally, when we pray we need to ask for peace. We can ask God to transform our lives into a gift of peace for others and ask that those for whom we pray receive it. A beautiful prayer attributed to Francis of Assisi, a thirteenth-century saint, begins with the request: "Lord, make me an instrument of thy peace; where there is hatred, let me sow love; where there is injury, pardon." When we pray like this, we open ourselves to the transforming power of the peace of the risen Christ. He gave this gift of *shalom* to a group of frightened disciples after his resurrection. "Peace be with you [*shalom*]" (John 20:19-21).

Prayer is personal but never private. When we pray we are always in communion with the body of Christ, the church, the community of all believers. In our prayers of petition and intercession, we ask for what we think we and others need but trust that God knows best. We ask openly and honestly out of our poverty, not as an attempt to control God. Moreover, when we ask for anything, we also make a deeper commitment to be faithful followers of Christ. As we present our petitions to God and ask for the coming of God's kingdom, we also commit ourselves to work for its realization to the best of our abilities.

Our prayers of petition and intercession are not a quiet activity but one full of energy and action. As we ask, we surrender; as we express our needs and hopes, we trust. There is nothing resigned about this form of prayer. It calls for faith, openness, and a deep commitment to work with God toward the coming of the kingdom for which we so earnestly pray.

DAILY EXERCISES

Read "Prayers of Petition and Intercession" before you begin the exercises. Keep your journal beside you to record your thoughts, questions, prayers, and insights. Prepare yourself by considering the meaning of the following quotation:

> All your love, your stretching out, your hope, your thirst, God is creating in you so that [God] may fill you . . . [God] is on the inside of the longing.[2]

Eph 3: 16-19

This week's exercises invite you to claim the yearnings of your heart in prayer and to join them with God's great yearning for you and for all people in Jesus Christ.

EXERCISE 1

Read Luke 11:9-13. For what do you typically pray? List some of your requests in your notebook or journal. Note your awareness of God's responses. What bearing do Jesus' words of guidance (*ask, search, knock*) have on your experience?

Devote at least ten minutes to your breath prayer. Record your experience in your notebook or journal. Continue using your breath prayer each day as often as you remember it.

EXERCISE 2

Read John 15:7. Note the conditions of this New Testament promise ("If you abide in me, and my words abide in you, ask. . . . "). When you ask God for something, is your attitude one of willfulness ("I am determined to continue to ask for what I want, no matter what!") or willingness ("I present my needs to God but am willing to yield to the persuasions of God's wisdom and love.")? Apply the conditions of John 15:7 to something you are seeking, perhaps your breath prayer. How are you challenged? In what ways does your prayer change?

Devote at least ten minutes to your breath prayer. Record your experience in your notebook or journal. Continue to use your breath prayer frequently through each day.

EXERCISE 3

Read Matthew 6:31-33 several times. To reflect on what it means to focus on the kingdom of God, draw a large circle on a page in your notebook or journal. Around the circumference, name "all these things" about which you are anxious. Now consider what Jesus' words, "strive first for the kingdom of God," mean for you. As you gain clarity about what this priority means to you, write the priority in the center of the circle. Reflect on how this priority could change your life over time.

Devote at least a few minutes to your breath prayer. Note any insights about the relationship of your breath prayer to your reflection on priorities.

EXERCISE 4

Read Colossians 1:9-12. Focus on the expansiveness of Paul's hope and prayer for his fellow Christians. Now write a letter to persons in your family, Sunday school class, or workplace expressing your prayer for them. In doing so, give the love of Christ in you full rein to express your highest hopes and passion for their spiritual well-being.

Devote several minutes to your breath prayer. See if you can naturally incorporate your prayer for others as expressed in your letter. Continue your breath prayer throughout the day, remembering Paul's words, "We have not ceased praying for you."

EXERCISE 5

Read Ephesians 6:18-20. These words imply both spontaneity and intentionality in praying for others. "Pray in the Spirit at all times." As you pray your breath prayer, pay attention to people and situations that rise spontaneously in your awareness. Welcome them into your prayer with the love of Christ. Offer them to God in love, trusting the Spirit to work out the specifics. Be open to the appearance of enemies, difficult people, and unexpected faces from long ago. Trust the Spirit to make your prayer a means by which God's love touches these people today.

"Keep alert and always persevere in supplication for all the saints." Experiment by making a list of people you feel committed to pray for regularly, if not daily. Add to it others for whom you feel special responsibility or concern. If the list becomes quite long, break it into seven segments, one for each day of the week. Beginning today, spend a few minutes lifting several of these people to God.

Let your breath prayer adapt to the flow of God's love. Remember to pray it frequently each day.

Remember to review the insights recorded in your notebook or journal for the week in preparation for the group meeting.

Part 3, Week 4
Praying As We Are

Carol and George have been married for fifteen years. They have served as youth ministers in their church for several months. Recently the pastor invited them to attend a conference on the importance of prayer given by a guest speaker. The speaker's words deeply touched them, and they decided to visit a prayer group to which some friends belonged.

The first night the group gathered, George was very excited. He anticipated meeting new people and talking to others about his prayer life. Carol, on the other hand, was having second thoughts about their decision and wondered whether she belonged in a prayer meeting at all.

The prayer community met regularly in the home of one of the members. Upon arrival, Carol and George were warmly welcomed by all present. After brief introductions, songs were sung, and a passage from scripture was read. Immediately someone began to thank and praise God for the word just shared; soon all joined in a spontaneous chorus of praise and thanksgiving. After a brief pause, one of the participants was moved to share a testimony of the change wrought in his life through an encounter with Jesus the previous year. More expressions of praise and thanksgiving for God's goodness and mercy followed this moving story. Soon afterward, the leader invited those present to offer some simple prayers of petition. When the prayer time concluded, the host and hostess asked everyone to stay for

refreshments and informal sharing about the meeting. George felt delighted, full of energy and enthusiasm. Carol was drained, over-whelmed, and could not wait to get home. Once in the car listening to George, Carol felt miserable and thought that surely she was less holy and pious than George. George was empathetic, encouraging her to be patient and to give herself time to become comfortable praying in a group. Neither Carol nor George understood the dynamics of their conversation and arrived home confused and frustrated.

Such situations occur frequently in our congregations. People respond in different ways to the same stimulus and experience. We tend to assume that one party is right and the other wrong or at least that one is more advanced than the other. In this case, Carol feels "less open to prayer" than George. She apparently assumes that he is more receptive to prayer than she is. Yet the opposite could also occur. Carol could argue that this group was not able to be silent and reflective for one minute and that prayers were too emotional and superficial. Must Carol try to enjoy the spontaneous prayer group? Should we as Christians strive for uniformity in our responses to God?

We sometimes feel discouraged because we do not pray like someone we love and admire. However, spiritual writers and guides have consistently warned against casting people into one mold. Many great saints and mystics have cautioned Christians against forcing others to follow one's own spiritual path. One modern teacher, Urban T. Holmes, has provided a brief overview of the variety and richness of the Christian spiritual experience in his book *A History of Christian Spirituality*. He lists two intersecting scales that result in a typology of Christian spirituality. Several authors have used and adapted Holmes's ideas to help people identify their natural style of spirituality. Corinne Ware in her book *Discover Your Spiritual Type* has developed the "Spirituality Wheel Selector" as an instrument to help individuals and congregations explore their preferences.

During this week we will use these and other sources to reflect on the four types of spirituality that result when we use the two intersecting scales. My hope is that this study will help us gain a better understanding of Carol and George's predicament.

The Horizontal Scale: Mystery/Revelation

As Christians, we believe that the all-transcendent God is ineffable and incomprehensible. The book of the prophet Isaiah reminds us: "My thoughts are not your thoughts, nor are your ways my ways, says the LORD. For as the heavens are higher than the earth, so are my ways higher than your ways and my thoughts than your thoughts" (Isa. 55:8-9). Simultaneously, we believe that all created things provide ways of knowing God. Paul writes, "Ever since the creation of the world his eternal power and divine nature, invisible though they are, have been understood and seen through the things he has made" (Rom. 1:20).

At first glance, these statements may appear contradictory. However, they reflect the whole mystery of the Christian God: the God who is with us, Immanuel, yet who remains wholly Other. The Christian tradition has always reflected these two ways of speaking about and relating to God: the way of mystery and the way of revelation.

The way of mystery emphasizes the great dissimilarities between God and creature. It calls for humble seeking and self-emptying in imitation of Christ's love. As a mode of prayer, the way of mystery exhorts the seeker to "leave behind . . . everything perceived and understood . . . and . . . to strive . . . toward union with him who is beyond all being and knowledge."[1] This translates into a prayer that does not rely on reason, senses, images, or symbols. It is an expression of Christian tradition described by one writer as "that of naked faith, through which one is led in poverty and great longing beyond all concepts and images into a deep hidden knowledge of our union with God in Christ."[2]

In contrast, the way of revelation emphasizes the similarities between God and creation and emphasizes God's incarnation in the person of Jesus. As a mode of prayer, it uses created things, reason, imagining, and feeling as means to relate to God who is revealed and knowable. The renowned thirteenth-century Christian saint Francis of Assisi clearly represents this type of spirituality. Francis had a deep reverence for all God's creatures and viewed communion with them as an encounter with God. For him, all creation was transparent as a sacrament of God's presence. Francis saw God in everything: in the earth, sun, moon, stars, and fire, and in his own physical illnesses, blindness, and, ultimately, in his encounter with "sister death." In his beloved poem of praise, "The Canticle of Creatures," he expressed a fraternal relationship with all that is.

The ways of mystery and revelation are not in competition with each other. They are to some degree complementary and could be placed at opposite ends of the same prayer spectrum. They are connected because the revelation of God is always linked to God's mystery and hiddenness. Moreover, one way is not more desirable than the other. Mystery emphasizes that nothing can fully capture or portray the reality of God, so it is acceptable to go to God in "nothingness." Revelation implies that every created thing shows something of the Divine, so it is acceptable to go to God through everything. Praying in the way of mystery aims to move us beyond sensory or mental awareness into a direct experience of union with God. Praying in the way of revelation looks for God in all things because all creatures are the expression of divine life and can therefore also lead to union with God. Both ways of prayer are solidly rooted in biblical spirituality and as such are valid options for the Christian spiritual seeker.

Where would we find Carol and George on this scale? From the little we know about them, it seems that George found God easily in the concrete testimonies of faith shared in the group. Perhaps Carol would have felt more comfortable if there had been some silent time that would have allowed her to enter into the mystery of God's presence in her preferred way. Is one better than the other?

The Vertical Scale: Mind/Heart

The second scale suggested by Urban T. Holmes[3] is the mind/heart scale. In our desire to know God, some Christians seek illumination of the mind, while others seek illumination of the heart. The former have a more rational or intellectual relationship with God. God to them is known through categories of thought such as goodness, love,

> *To know God is to know one's own true Self, the ground of one's being. So prayer is an intensely human experience in which our eyes are opened and we begin to see more clearly our own true nature.*
>
> —Kenneth Leech

truth. The latter seek more to have an affective or feeling relationship with God. The tension between mind and heart preferences is probably one more easily identified in our congregations. Have you ever heard members of your church strongly advocate the need for sermons with better content or the formation of Bible study groups? Do you find others who feel that the quality of fellowship or inspired singing in the church is more important than any sermon? Is one right and the other wrong? We know that both are needed to help a congregation grow. Since we will always find people at both ends of the scale, the challenge is to look at these poles as integral parts of one whole reality and not as opposites in competition. In my own ministry I spend considerable time helping people work through the tension caused by these two positions. For some, having an intellectual insight about God or an awareness of God's will is the central element of their faith. For others, feeling God's presence and loving care is the core of the religious experience. Again, is one better than the other?

I believe our emotions—all of them—belong in our prayers....Our prayers represent not just what we say but who we are, with all our complex longings and feelings.
—Timothy Jones

In the case presented in this chapter, could George's personality be more heart-centered and Carol's more mind-oriented? Might the emotions displayed in the group have made Carol uncomfortable?

Understanding our preferences enables us to recognize and revere the various ways each person reflects God's image. This understanding, in turn, suggests different approaches to prayer. What helps one person's prayer life may hinder another person's spiritual development. We need to be careful about casting people into one mold and assuming that one spiritual path or style of prayer, if helpful to us, must be helpful to everyone else. We need to remember that each person is a unique image of God, created with specific personality traits and preferences that are to be honored as we respond to God's initiative in prayer. Paul writes to the early Christians: "For as in one body we have many members, and not all the members have the same function, so we, who are many, are one body in Christ....We have gifts that differ according to the grace given to us" (Rom. 12:4-6).

If our gifts differ and we play different roles in the body, would it not make sense to surmise that we all relate to God in different ways?

Four Types of Spirituality

When we allow the lines represented by these two spectrums to intersect, we see the quadrants designated by Holmes as four types of spirituality. The following diagram comes from Corinne Ware's book in which she expands on Holmes's understandings of spiritual types.[4]

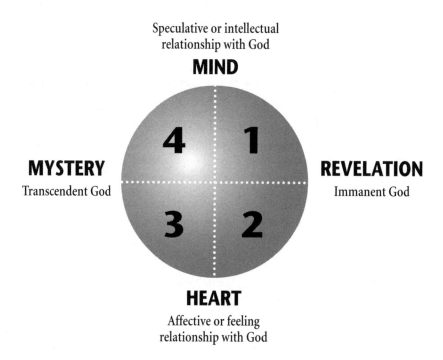

Speculative or intellectual
relationship with God

MIND

MYSTERY
Transcendent God

REVELATION
Immanent God

HEART
Affective or feeling
relationship with God

Type 1: Revelation/Mind. This type of spirituality favors theological reflection on concepts such as the Incarnation, God's love, or ethical issues. Christians in this group enjoy study groups and concrete ways of deepening the understanding of their faith. The gift of this type is theological reflection on the content of the Christian faith. The danger is what Holmes calls "rationalism" or the excessive intellectualization of the spiritual life.

Type 2: Revelation/Heart. The members of this group favor a more affective, charismatic spirituality. Their way to God is not the rational mind but the experience of the heart. Their gift includes warmth, enthusiasm, and energy in religious expression. The danger is becoming so convinced of the greater value of their felt experience that they tend to dismiss theological reflection as irrelevant.

Type 3: Mystery/Heart. Ware considers this type the most mystical. This group desires union with God, the Holy One. The gift of this type is an inspirational and uplifting spirituality that challenges others to be totally open to God. The danger is that this type of spirituality may become overly passive or retreat from reality.

Type 4: Mystery/Mind. Ware considers this the smallest group and, thus, the most difficult to describe. People who embody this type tend to be idealistic and radical in a desire to witness to God's reign. They have a passion for transforming society.[5] For them, prayer, theology, and action are one. They are intellectual visionaries, and their gift is precisely their vision of the ideal and their commitment to it. Their temptation is to an extreme moralistic vision. This group can dismiss those who do not support their "cause" with their same single-mindedness.

Identifying our spiritual type is not meant to box us into a given category. As Ware interprets Holmes, "once we have found where we fall within the total circle, we then have opportunity to grow by (1) acknowledging and strengthening our present gifts, (2) growing toward our opposite quadrant, and (3) appreciating more perceptively the quadrants on either side of our dominant type."[6] It is important to avoid stereotyping or oversimplifying the spiritual journey. No scales or schema can adequately explain the mystery of God and the mystery of the human response to God's initiative. The God of Jesus Christ remains beyond our ability to describe and eludes our feeble attempts to control, possess, or define. Paradoxically, in Jesus, the Otherness of God has joined creation. The late German theologian Karl Rahner expressed this eloquently:

> [Lord,] You must adapt Your word to my smallness, so that it can enter into the tiny dwelling of my finiteness.... You must make Your own

some human word, for that's the only kind I can comprehend....O Infinite God, You have actually willed to speak such a word to me!...You have come to me in a human word. For You, the Infinite, are the God of Our Lord Jesus Christ.[7]

This belief in the Incarnation encourages us to try to understand our humanity and to discover the richness of the various ways in which God wishes to be revealed to us.

When we look at Jesus as presented in the Gospels, we find that at various times in his life Jesus reflected different styles of prayer. He certainly emptied himself of everything in order to make his will one with God's will. He also saw God's presence in everyone and in everything: the children, the lilies of the field, the generosity of the poor widow, the faith of the centurion. Jesus knew the scriptures and used them to outline for his followers the radical demands of discipleship. But Jesus also wept when Lazarus died and was deeply moved over the city of Jerusalem. Jesus prayed alone, away from the disciples, and also encouraged them to pray with him. To be one with his Father was the deepest joy of Jesus' heart, and he desired this oneness for us all "that they may all be one. As you, Father, are in me and I am in you, may they also be in us" (John 17:21).

As Christians, we believe that "where the Spirit of the Lord is, there is freedom" (2 Cor. 3:17). Jesus lived fully in such freedom. Each Gospel writer describes Jesus in a unique manner and helps us to see how Jesus revealed the various dimensions of God. By providing such a rich variety of images of God, the New Testament invites us to enter the mystery of the God who eludes all definition and yet has chosen to walk with us as a fellow pilgrim.

The gift given by Jesus after the resurrection is *shalom*: peace, harmony, unity, integrity within God's own being (John 20:19). Unity means not uniformity but oneness in the midst of diversity. There is diversity in the Trinity. There is diversity in Jesus. There is diversity in the Gospel writers. There were diverse languages at Pentecost, and yet the gift of the Spirit was unity in the diversity. "Indeed, the body does not consist of one member but of many" (1 Cor. 12:14). There are different prayer styles, various ways to become present to God's

Breathe in the breath of the Spirit. Be free. Be simple. Prayer is a perfectly natural relationship between God, who loved you first, and you who try to love [God] back.

—Catherine de Hueck Doherty

presence in our lives. The challenge is to understand one's individual style better and, in doing so, become free to appreciate and respect other approaches.

Carol may never understand why George liked the prayer group so much. George certainly does not comprehend why Carol did not enjoy such a wonderful experience. The hope is that as they develop spiritually, they will come to revere and appreciate the differences between them and the rich variety of gifts among members of the body of Christ.

DAILY EXERCISES

Read the chapter for Week 4 titled "Praying As We Are." Be sure to note any questions or insights in your journal. Begin your exercises by reflecting on the following quotation:

> Pray as you can, not as you can't.[8]

With Exercises 1–4, you will experience prayer forms that are expressive of the four spiritual types discussed in this week's reading. We could characterize the types as head (revelation/mind), heart (revelation/heart), mystic (mystery/heart), and active (mystery/mind).

EXERCISE 1: "HEAD" SPIRITUALITY

Read John 3:16. Think about what this verse means. Paraphrase the verse in a sentence or two that capture the essence of its meaning for you. Then write a prayer to God that expresses your thoughts about what God has done for us and why we need what God has given to us.

EXERCISE 2: "HEART" SPIRITUALITY

Read John 3:16. List several people you love and those you have difficulty loving. Read the verse slowly for each person on your list, personalizing this verse as an expression of God's love for him or her: "For God so loved (name) that he gave his only Son, so that everyone who believes in him may not perish but may have eternal life." Include yourself. Pause to add your prayer for each person and to pray for what you need in order to love that person. Notice any changes in you as you affirm God's love for the person. Decide how you are going to express God's love and your love to the people on your list. Record your experience.

EXERCISE 3: "MYSTIC" SPIRITUALITY

Read John 3:16. Repeat this verse prayerfully as a way of focusing on God. Open your spirit to the loving attitude of Jesus Christ who allowed himself to be given for our salvation. Give yourself to the flow of God's boundless love for the whole world, a love that flows in and through you. As people and situations come to mind, bring them into the flow and allow them to be washed in God's boundless love. Finally, carry some part of John 3:16 with you in your daily activities as a way of practicing openness to God's love. Record your experience.

EXERCISE 4: "ACTIVE" SPIRITUALITY

Read John 3:16. Today you will not be seeking to understand, feel, or contemplate the love described in this verse. Rather, be a living prayer today, an expression of God's sacrificial love. As you are able, take a walk through your house, your workplace, or your neighborhood. Bless everyone and everything you see with the words, "For God so loved the world...." Where do you see a need for God's love? Consider what Jesus would do in that situation, and choose a way to embody God's love in action. Record your experience.

EXERCISE 5

Read 1 Thessalonians 5:16-19. Take a moment to reflect on what these verses say about what it means to live prayerfully. Devote most of your time to the practice of being present to God and remaining in God's love. Use whatever approach helps you and seems most natural. During your last few minutes, reflect in your journal on these questions: (a) How am I experiencing God's presence and my presence to God these days? (b) What am I discovering about my way of praying and relating to God? (c) What helps me pray, and what gets in the way?

Review your journal entries for the week in preparation for the group meeting.

Part 3, Week 5
Psalms, the Prayer Book of the Bible

What feelings do you experience most frequently—gratitude, wonder, joy, boredom, anger, despair? Do you ever feel ashamed of your feelings of hatred or rage? What do you do with these strong emotions? How do you express them and how do you feel about them in relation to your faith?

Whatever our feelings, we will certainly find them expressed in the Psalms. This book, a collection of 150 prayers of the people of Israel, are meant to be sung accompanied by musical instruments. The Psalms are the poetry and music of the Jewish people at prayer and are deeply grounded in Hebrew spirituality.

The God of Israel is definitely interested in creation. The Hebrew scriptures tell of a God who breaks into history and is the Lord of history, a God who communicates with the people and pursues them. The Hebrew God is profoundly involved in human affairs. God appears to Abram and offers to make a covenant with him (Gen. 17:1-2). God heeds Rachel's prayer and opens her womb (Gen. 30:22). God speaks to Moses, assuring him that that the cries of the people have been heard, and they will be delivered from the Egyptians (Exod. 3:7-8). The God of the Israelites can also be convinced to change directions. When God threatens to destroy Sodom and Gomorrah, Abraham persuades God to spare the city of Sodom for the sake of ten righteous people living in it (Gen. 18:22-23).

The God of Israel desires an intimate relationship with the people. In spite of Israel's idolatry, God lures her and brings her into the wilderness to speak tenderly to her. God hopes that in the desert Israel will remember the days of her youth when she came out of the land of Egypt, and, there, once again return to God. Using powerful symbolic imagery, the prophet Hosea proclaims that God longs for the day when Israel will call God her husband, and God will take her for his wife forever (Hos. 2:14-20). The God of Israel is a gracious God who longs to enter into a passionate relationship of covenantal love with the people. In Hebrew spirituality God is the omnipotent creator and judge but also the companion in battle and the jealous lover.

The Psalms emerge within the context of this personal relationship. Because of the deep conviction that God was among them, protecting, loving, rebuking, and guiding, Jewish people freely went to God with their feelings. They prayed in their anger, hatred, and frustration; they talked to their ever-present God of the pain of their exile, their powerlessness before the enemy, and the depth of their fears. They also went to God in their triumphs and with hearts full of gratitude for graces received. Every human emotion found expression in the Psalms.

This week we take a new look at this old collection of prayers and explore their role and significance in the prayer of contemporary Christians.

> *People are driven to such poignant prayer and song as are found in the Psalter precisely by* experiences of dislocation and relocation. *It is experiences of being overwhelmed, nearly destroyed, and surprisingly given life which empower us to pray and sing.*
>
> —Walter Brueggemann

The Book of Psalms

The Book of Psalms covers a period of more than six hundred years in the history of the people of Israel. These 150 songs praise the God of creation and depict the struggles of God's people through the period of the patriarchs to the time after the Babylonian exile ended. The oldest psalms were prayed by the communities in which they originated, and they were later adapted and used in different situations the people faced. The psalms were set to the accompaniment of musical instruments, usually stringed instruments, such as a lyre or zither. They were gradually collected and initially remained unnamed, due to the large variety of material. Eventually, the Book of Psalms was written and became the foremost prayer book of the people of Israel. The original collection of the Psalms in Hebrew was completed by the third century B.C.E., though many of the individual psalms were much older. The Greek translation dates from the mid-third century B.C.E. (with later revisions) and is the version most used by the writers of the New Testament. Most modern translations come directly from the Hebrew text. When the first Christian communities used the Psalms as part of their prayer, they reinterpreted them in light of Jesus' life, death, and resurrection.

The Gospels present Jesus as the chief pray-er of the psalms. According to Matthew, Jesus spoke in parables to fulfill what had been spoken through the prophet: "I will open my mouth to speak in parables" (Matt. 13:35). In this instance he is quoting Psalm 78:2. In the same Gospel, Jesus uses Psalm 6:8 when he delivers his angry words against religious hypocrites who say, "Lord, Lord," but do not do the will of the Father: "Go away from me, you evildoers" (Matt. 7:23). The Gospels of Matthew, Mark, and Luke quote Psalm 110:1 to indicate that Jesus is the Lord of whom David spoke in the Book of Psalms (Matt. 22:44; 26:64; Mark 12:36; 14:62; Luke 20:42-43). According to Matthew, Jesus' final words from the cross are taken from Psalm 22:1: "My God, my God, why have you forsaken me?" (Matt. 27:46). In these words we hear the same sense of abandonment experienced by the psalmist of ancient Israel: "Why are you so far from helping me, from the words of my groaning? O my God, I cry by day, but you do not answer; and by night, but find no rest" (Psalm 22:1-2). The Gospel of Luke records other words spoken by Jesus from the cross: "Father, into your hands I commend my spirit" (Luke 23:46). These words parallel those of Psalm 31:5.

Today there are moments when we can identify with the psalmist just as Jesus did. We move from despair to surrender, from telling God how abandoned we feel to placing our lives in God's hands. The Gospels make other references to the psalms reflecting the significance of these ancient hymns in early Christian worship. As Christians, we are invited to let the psalms enrich our lives, to be our poems and

songs. These ancient hymns enable us to turn our strongest feelings and life experiences into prayers.

Division of the Psalms

Traditionally, the book has been divided into five parts, probably in imitation of the Pentateuch, the first five books of the Hebrew Scriptures:

Book I:	Psalms 1–41	Basic songs of worship
Book II:	Psalms 42–72	Songs of national concerns, emphasizing deliverance and redemption
Book III:	Psalms 73–89	Also hymns of national concerns, emphasizing worship and the sanctuary
Book IV:	Psalms 90–106	Songs of praise, with the themes of wilderness and wandering
Book V:	Psalms 107–150	Songs of praise

Within these main divisions we find subdivisions that make the psalms easier to understand for the contemporary reader. For example, there are Pilgrimage Psalms (such as 120–134) used in the annual journey to the Temple in Jerusalem during the high holy days; Individual Lament Psalms (such as 3–7; 12; 13; 22; 25–28; 35; 38–40; 42–43; 51; 54–57); and Communal Lament Psalms, in which the nation rather than an individual laments (such as 44; 60; 74; 79–80; 90; 123). There are also individual and communal Psalms of Thanksgiving, Psalms of Praise, Royal Psalms, and Wisdom Psalms. Contemporary scholars differ on methods of classification and on the exact name given to each subgroup. Nevertheless, the Book of Psalms remains a treasure of prayers that explores the full range of human emotions and experience and that places Yahweh, the God of the covenant, at the center of the human journey.

Difficulties Praying the Psalms Today

Often the psalms play a marginal role in the prayer of contemporary Christians. I have identified three difficulties encountered when approaching the Book of Psalms:

— WRONG

Old vs New Testam't

1. Resistance to praying with our feelings.
2. Images of God that seem to contradict the God revealed by Jesus.
3. Harsh language and attitudes that appear at odds with the Gospel message.

Resistance to praying with our feelings. We live in a culture that applauds self-control and is suspicious of the expression of strong emotion. There is a covert assumption that one must especially avoid any expression of powerful, negative feelings. In mainline U.S. culture, this is particularly true when it comes to men showing deep sadness, grief, or fear, and women expressing anger or hatred. It is widely accepted that "men do not cry," and women are expected to be "nice and sweet." Even for people who have no trouble with sadness or fear, the psalms of rage and anger present a serious problem. This prevailing attitude attains new depths among many Christians who mistakenly believe that in their time of prayer they should be composed and calm. Yet several psalms demonstrate the acceptability of praying with our grief and anger, even when directed to God (Psalms 35; 109; and 137), as in Jesus' cries from the cross (Matt. 27:46).

> Praying with the psalms can be a liberating and healing experience for many of us. Expressing our brokenness, fears, joys, and anger when we pray, far from being an obstacle and a cause for anxiety, can become transforming moments when our deepest and strongest emotions become prayers. What better place to express our deepest feelings than in the presence of our loving God!

Images of God that seem to contradict the God revealed by Jesus. Frequently, Christians complain that in the psalms they encounter a God of fear, a God who loves only some and wishes the destruction of all enemies. This God resembles a crusader out to exterminate evildoers

The wide range of expression in the Psalter—the anger and pain of lament, the anguished self-probing of confession, the grateful fervor of thanksgiving, the ecstatic joy of praise—allows us to bring our whole lives before God.

—Kathleen Norris

who oppose God's plan. Such an attitude seems to contradict Jesus' words, "Do not resist an evildoer.…Love your enemies and pray for those who persecute you" (Matt. 5:39, 44). The God of Jesus "makes his sun rise on the evil and on the good, and sends rain on the righteous and on the unrighteous" (Matt. 5:45). How do we reconcile the vengeful God of the psalms with the compassionate father in the parable of the prodigal son (Luke 15:11-32)? How can we imagine the Christian God taking sides in a war and destroying one group so that the other may win?

To understand the psalmist's prayer, we attempt to place ourselves in the historical and theological context in which the psalms were written. The concept of "chosen people" is integral to Hebrew spirituality. Yahweh, the God of gods, the God of creation and of all that is, was specifically the God of Abraham, Isaac, and Jacob. Jews believed that they were special and that God was guiding them and preserving their life as a tiny, vulnerable nation. As the different psalms were written over a long period of time, they not only portrayed the struggle of the people of Israel but also reflected varied and evolving human understandings of who God was.

Is this pattern so different from today? As Christians in relationship with the living God, we perceive our God in many different ways throughout our lives. For some, God is a just judge; for others, God is always loving and compassionate. Many see God as distantly omnipotent and omniscient. Others see God as walking hand in hand with them in the midst of their daily routines. At moments in our lives we experience God as friend and companion. We often see God as our protector, defender, and deliverer. But God may also seem mysteriously absent in our crises. The question of who God is has been part of the human quest from ancient times. The Book of Psalms offers us the Jewish understanding of the Israelites' God and invites us to approach this God with the entire gamut of human emotions, just as Jesus and the early Christians did.

Harsh language and attitudes that appear at odds with the Gospel message. When Christians today read Psalm 137, they frequently feel revulsion; something turns inside and cries, "This is wrong!" How can we possibly pray, as the psalmist does, for a blessing upon those who will dash babies against a rock (v. 9)? How can we call this kind of writing the Word of God?

The psalms frequently reflect the emotional state of a people suffering dehumanizing experiences. The people, in their pain, call for divine justice but refrain from human vengeance: "Repay them…according to the evil of their deeds.…Because they do not regard the works of the LORD, or the work of his hands, he will break them down and build them up no more" (Ps. 28:4-5). The psalmist prays for divine justice on those whom he considers evil in the eyes of God. This evil is frequently defined as a direct injustice or attack on the people the Lord has chosen to be God's own. Thus, the psalmist considers any attack on the Israelites an attack against God. The hatred, pain, and bitterness of the Israelites' suffering under the Babylonians and others find expression in the "harsh" psalms. These are sometimes referred to as the Imprecatory Psalms, which call down God's curses on the enemy. Over the centuries, many Christians have identified the "enemies" referred to in the psalms as forces and powers that try to pull us away from God and attack us when we resist. This understanding may open up new insights as we pray with the psalms.

Finding a Home in the Psalms

The psalms encourage contemporary Christians to allow their feelings to find a home in prayer. God does not expect us to approach prayer only when we feel calm and collected. We approach our God as we are, with raw feelings and emotions, and allow God's embrace to touch, heal, or affirm them. In prayer we express the resentment we feel against someone who has hurt us: "In my distress I cry to the LORD…: Deliver me, O LORD, from lying lips, from a deceitful tongue" (Ps. 120:1-2). In moments of depression and despair we exclaim, "Out of the depths I cry to you, O LORD…hear my voice!" (Ps. 130:1-2). When feelings of gratitude well up inside our hearts, we say, "I love the LORD, because he has heard my voice and my supplications" (Ps. 116:1).

But the continuing appeal of the psalms is not only that they help us articulate the full range of our experiences and emotions; they offer us that help in the context of prayer. The psalms are primarily human speech to God. They arose out of the life of a praying community, Israel, responding to its experiences in the context of relationship to God.…It is not merely life itself, but life lived in relationship to, and in conversation with, God that permeates the psalms.

—Larry R. Kalajainen

In moments when we feel abandoned and when God seems silent, we pray, "Incline your ear to my cry. For my soul is full of troubles....O LORD, why do you cast me off? Why do you hide your face from me?" (Ps. 88:2-3, 14). As we bring our feelings to God in prayer, we acknowledge God's presence in them, and we open up to hear what God may be trying to say through them. Feelings become our companions on the journey, and we stop seeing them as enemies. In the safe space created by prayer, we welcome our feelings, accept them, and then, with childlike trust, turn them over to our loving God.

DAILY EXERCISES

Read the chapter for Week 5 titled "Psalms, the Prayer Book of the Bible." Record your questions and comments in your journal. Reflect on the following quotation as you begin your daily exercises:

> Jesus understood who he was and what he was called to become by praying the psalms....The psalms, infused with this presence of Christ, make accessible and actual for us the full range of Jesus' experience. In praying the psalms, we enter into that world of meaning and find our own wilderness sojourn illuminated and clarified. In praying the psalms we pass through our own hearts to the heart of God as revealed in Jesus' inner life.[1]

In these exercises, you will find a challenge to pray the Psalms with candor and, in so doing, to enter more fully into the vitality of Jesus' life with God.

EXERCISE 1

Read Psalm 8. Join with Jesus Christ in praying this psalm. Let each verse lead you to celebrate who you are before God, the magnificence of creation, and the human calling. What verses do you imagine spoke to Jesus as he prayed this psalm? What verses connect most deeply with you? Commit a few special verses to memory. Repeat them as you go about your daily tasks as a way to praise God.

EXERCISE 2

Read Psalm 10 aloud. Reflect on what circumstances might have inspired someone to write this psalm. Remember that "the poor" might refer to anyone who feels powerless or disregarded by those who have power. Try to pray this psalm as Jesus may have prayed it. Imagine the persons with whom Jesus may have identified as he prayed these words. Do you have any difficulty in praying this psalm? Identify with "the poor" in your own community as you pray the psalm again. Offer your prayer in the spirit of Jesus. Record your insights and experience.

EXERCISE 3

Read Psalm 22:1-11 and meditate on it verse by verse. As you read verses 1-5, identify the parts of your life in which you feel God's absence (vv. 1-2). Discover also the parts of yourself that want to trust God nevertheless (vv. 3-5). Express both feelings to God. Listen to God in the silence.

Meditate on verses 1-11, remembering that Jesus prayed this psalm as he hung on the cross. Sit before a picture of Jesus, a cross, or an icon. Imagine Jesus' human feelings and questions. How does the psalm illumine your ability to identify with Jesus and his humanness? What does the psalm suggest about Jesus' experience of having faith in the extreme moments of suffering and aloneness? Write your thoughts in your journal.

EXERCISE 4

Read Psalm 46. Imagine praying this psalm in the company of Jesus and all the saints who lived such faith, especially in times of trouble. Personalize verses 2-3. Bring to mind the things that can and do shake your faith as you pray the words, "Therefore we will not fear." Record your insights and experience.

EXERCISE 5

Find a psalm that gives voice to how you feel at this time about your life and your relationship with God. Write a paraphrase of the psalm that captures the prayer of your heart. What do you imagine was happening to the psalmist when he wrote the original words of the psalm? Read the psalm and your paraphrase, and pray the words once more, united in spirit with the psalmist.

Remember to review your journal entries for the week in preparation for the group meeting.

Exploring Contemplative Prayer

One of the most colorful stories in the New Testament is without a doubt the story of Martha and Mary (Luke 10:38-42). Luke tells us of the day when a woman named Martha welcomed Jesus into her home. Martha had a sister named Mary who sat at the Lord's feet and listened to what he was saying. Meanwhile her sister, Martha, kept busy with many household tasks, which distracted her. Finally Martha came to Jesus and complained that her sister, Mary, had left her to do all the work by herself. Would he tell her to offer some help? According to Luke, Jesus answered with the familiar words: "Martha, Martha, you are worried and distracted by many things; there is need of only one thing. Mary has chosen the better part, which will not be taken away from her."

The Gospel story does not explain what this "better part" is; consequently, it has become the subject of countless sermons and reflections. One of the most common interpretations of this passage declares Martha a "busybody" activist and Mary a contemplative example in her attentiveness to Jesus. Those who explain the story in this fashion frequently maintain that Jesus clearly exalted being over doing, prayer over service, contemplation over action. Anyone intentionally walking the Christian path knows of the ever-present tension between these two polarities. Throughout twenty centuries of

Excuse for NOT helping

Christianity, various schools of spirituality have emphasized one or the other while maintaining that both contemplation and action are integral components of the Christian journey.

This week we focus on contemplation and contemplative prayer and their significance in the lives of Christians today.

Contemplation

If contemplation is the "better part" to which Jesus referred in the Martha and Mary story, he was certainly not speaking of Mary's sitting in contrast to Martha's movement. Martha's problem was not her work in the kitchen or her desire to be a gracious hostess. Rather, Jesus pointed out that she was worried and distracted by many things, not the least of which was her resentment toward her sister. Martha missed the point, not because she was serving, but because she lost sight of the "better part": Jesus' presence in her home. I do not think that Jesus meant for Martha to stop preparing the meal; instead, he meant for her to open the eyes and the ears of her heart to be present to him. Upon Jesus' arrival, Mary gave him her total attention. In contrast, Martha engaged in many tasks in a self-preoccupied manner that took her awareness away from Jesus' presence.

In this context, we may define contemplation as an awareness of God's presence and action. It means seeing reality as God sees it. It means being able to see God in everything and everything in God. When we live in a contemplative way, the whole creation becomes a sacrament of God's presence, an icon through which we encounter the divine. Most of us have experienced such moments of total transparency. At times a sunset over the ocean or the song of a bird or the laughter of a child takes us beyond what our senses perceive into the very mystery of God.

In truth, all Christians are called to contemplation, as evidenced in the Fourth Gospel. John, more than any other New Testament writer, underlines the oneness of Jesus with God, especially in chapters 14–17. Before his arrest, Jesus prays that the disciples might be one as the Father and he are one (John 17:22). This union with God is

Only when we are able to "let go" of everything within us, all desire to see, to know, to taste and to experience the presence of God, do we truly become able to experience that presence with the overwhelming conviction and reality that revolutionize our entire inner life.

—Thomas Merton

the deepest expression of contemplation—Jesus' prayer for everyone! Therefore, every person must have the capacity to be contemplative. Why, then, do some Christians believe that contemplation is beyond them, reserved for only a few?

One answer to this dilemma may lie in the various ways in which Christians understand contemplative prayer.

Contemplative Prayer

In popular circles, persons often use the words *contemplation, meditation,* and *mysticism* interchangeably. Consequently, many persons are unclear about the meaning of contemplative prayer. To confuse matters further, there is a subtle belief that to pray contemplatively, one has to be an otherworldly eccentric who experiences visions and other mystical phenomena. If you consider contemplative prayer as out of reach, it is time to look again at your understanding of this way of prayer.

In simple terms, contemplative prayer is "a way of making oneself aware of the presence of God who is always there."[1] It differs from meditation, which involves reasoning, words, and images. In true contemplative prayer, one abides in mystery, open to being taken by God in love along a way one cannot know. Throughout the history of Christianity, spiritual guides have regarded contemplative prayer as an encounter with the "unknowing." Because intuition and awareness rather than thinking are central to this experience, such prayer tends to be unitive; we find ourselves—our true selves—in God.

One of the obstacles blocking our contemplation is the inclination to displace the deepest longing of our hearts onto external possessions. Our culture lures us with promises of fulfillment and personal realization; all we have to do is drive a certain model of car or wear designer clothes. If our investments are solid and we manage to be debt free, we will have peace. Advertising and conventional wisdom promise satisfaction if we submit to the gods of the market economy. Surely our society makes it hard to live from one's center! But external things cannot satisfy the soul. As Augustine wrote, a prominent quality of the

The most fundamental step I believe we can take toward opening our spiritual heart is to open our longing for God: our yearning for God's fullness in us and the world, through and beyond every desire we may have. That longing is placed deep in us as a reflection of God's wondrous, loving desire to be full in us.

—Tilden H. Edwards

human spirit is its restlessness: "You have formed us for yourself, and our hearts are restless till they find rest in you."[2]

Another cultural value that forms an obstacle to contemplation is the rugged individualism of those "brave" enough to try to make it on their own. This attitude makes contemplative prayer sound like a foreign concept. Contemplative prayer acknowledges that we cannot make it on our own; we cannot force an experience of God's presence dwelling within us, no matter how hard we try. Rather, we pray by believing that we are God's beloved and that God dwells within us, already united with us if we only open up to that awareness. Moreover, we believe that God freely loves us and that our baptism and faith have equipped us to experience this mystery of undeserved and unearned love. In contemplative prayer we listen to and see reality through the Spirit who dwells within us (Rom. 8:9; 1 Cor. 2:6-13).

Teresa of Avila, a Spanish mystic of the sixteenth century, saw that the journey of the soul to God began with the soul's remembrance of its true identity. She wrote, "I don't find anything comparable to the magnificent beauty of a soul and its marvelous capacity. Indeed, our intellects, however keen, can hardly comprehend it, just as they cannot comprehend God; but He Himself says that He created us in His own image and likeness."[3] We often forget this deepest identity when we pay attention to the many voices of our culture, but in prayer we are able to recover the sense of our identity as children of God.

In chapters 11–22 of the book of her *Life* (*Vida*), Teresa explains the soul's friendship with God by using the allegory of a garden. In the soul's garden, we do not need to plant seeds or pull up weeds because God has already done that. We simply need to water it, and the water is prayer. She insists that it is only with God's help that we "strive like good gardeners to get the plants to grow."[4] Our task may appear simple, but it is not always easy. The many cares of our lives, Martha's "worries and distractions," often become obstacles to our oneness with God.

During Week 4 of this unit on prayer, we reflected on two of the ways we speak about and relate to God: the way of mystery and the way of revelation. In more ancient terms, the way of mystery is called *apophatic* and the way of revelation is called *kataphatic*. This week we call again upon the wisdom of our tradition in order to gain a deeper understanding of contemplative prayer.

Approaches to Contemplative Prayer

Both ways of knowing God can help us understand contemplative prayer. *Apophatic* and *kataphatic* are Greek terms that describe two ways of entering contemplative prayer: One employs thoughts and images and is called the way of revelation (kataphatic way); the other is the way of mystery (apophatic way), which transcends ideas, thoughts, and symbols and enters, through love, into God's mystery.

Ignatius of Loyola (described in Part 2, page 46) was a man of deep contemplative prayer and a strong proponent of the kataphatic way. In his *Spiritual Exercises*, he encourages the use of imagination, feelings, senses, reason, will, and memory to enter the experience on which we meditate. He suggests that we place ourselves imaginatively in the scripture passage ("composition of place") in order to see, hear, smell, taste, and touch the people and places described there. Ignatius also suggests that we use the imagination to become active participants in the Bible story. This switch from rational to imaginative activity can make us more receptive to a deeper personal knowledge of Christ. At the end of the *Exercises*, Ignatius continues to offer ways to experience being at one with Christ in his passion and glory. He describes a contemplative prayer in which one moves beyond imagining Jesus' thoughts or feelings in the Gospel story to developing a sense of personal union with him. The Ignatian method's strength is its ability to immerse the entire person—body and soul—in profound Christian truths. Through prayer experiences based on Christ's life, Ignatius reveals how images and symbols become transparent to the mystery of God's self-giving love.

The apophatic approach emphasizes that no idea, thought, or symbol can fully reach God as God is. Several significant writers, including the anonymous author of *The Cloud of Unknowing* (fourteenth-century England), John of the Cross (sixteenth-century Spain),

and Thomas Merton (twentieth-century United States) have interpreted this way. *The Cloud*, a clear, concise book on the nature of apophatic prayer, urges its readers to enter into the kind of prayer where one is at home in a "dark cloud" beyond all thoughts and images. This author, along with many others in the Christian tradition, warns that no technique can bring about this experience and that contemplation is ultimately God's gift. He suggests a method that is now called "centering prayer." Those who choose this prayer style use a meaningful word (such as *Jesus, God, Love*) and then release any distracting thoughts or images in order to center attention on the reality behind the word. In centering prayer, as in any other apophatic method, one seeks to go beyond all words, thoughts, and images and to enter the center of one's being, awaiting the gift of total awareness of God's presence within.

These approaches to prayer offer two different ways to grow in the soul's friendship with God of which Teresa of Avila spoke. A practical woman and also a gifted contemplative, Teresa wrote extensively, presenting primarily the way of revelation. Yet one can see both approaches in her work. Regardless of one's preferred approach, contemplation in the Christian tradition is understood as an awareness of God's presence beyond thoughts and images. This experience is the product not of our efforts or merits, but of our faithful response to God's grace. In the kataphatic tradition such awareness comes through the transparency of everything; in the apophatic approach it comes through forgetting and "unknowing." Both approaches aim to free us from the false self in order to find the true self in God.

The Fruits of Contemplative Prayer

We have seen that contemplation is the work of love—not our love for God but God's love for us. The Christian God is a relational God who desires all to share in that love: "If we love one another, God lives in us, and his love is perfected in us" (1 John 4:12). Jesus experienced this union to the fullest and desired it for us all. Yet he further promised, "Those who abide in me and I in them bear much fruit" (John

My secret is very simple: I pray. Through prayer I become one in love with Christ. I realize that praying to him is loving him.... The poor who live in the slums of the world are the suffering Christ...and through them God shows me his true face. For me, prayer means being united to the will of God twenty-four hours a day, to live for him, through him, and with him.

—Mother Teresa

15:5). True contemplation leads not to self-absorption but to the emptying of oneself on behalf of others. Teresa of Avila wisely taught her nuns: "You may think that as a result [of the union with God] the soul will be outside itself and so absorbed that it will be unable to be occupied with anything else. On the contrary, the soul is much more occupied than before with everything pertaining to the service of God."[5] It is necessary that Christians honestly examine the fruits of their contemplative prayer. The following list may assist in this reflection.

True contemplative prayer leads to

- the experience of God within, which silences other voices that deny our human dignity.
- the awareness of God's infinite love for us through no merit of our own.
- self-knowledge that leads to humility; that is, to walk in truth.
- compassion and works of mercy.
- peace.
- freedom.

Martha and Mary live within each one of us. Yes, we would love to sit close to Jesus and put aside all distractions and cares simply to be with him. Yet the Martha within worries and gets distracted by many needless anxieties. The purpose of contemplative prayer is to take us deep within to the place where God is, in order to rest in God and become more aware of God's radical transforming love for us. When we allow time and space for this gift to be revealed, our various tasks become acts of love, and our suffering becomes redemptive. We will have chosen to dwell with Jesus in the heart of God. We will have chosen the "better part," and it will not be taken away from us.

The spiritual life can be lived in as many ways as there are people. What is new is that we have moved from the many things to the kingdom of God. What is new is that we are set free from the compulsions of our world and have set our hearts on the only necessary thing.

—Henri J. M. Nouwen

DAILY EXERCISES

Read the chapter for Week 6, "Exploring Contemplative Prayer," and note in your journal your insights, learnings, and questions.

One characteristic of progress in the spiritual life is an increasing reliance on God in our daily living and our praying. An increasing reliance on God is sometimes accompanied by a preference or even a sense of call toward a simpler form of prayer that emphasizes our words and thoughts less and God's communication with us and presence in us more. "I have given up all my non-obligatory devotions and prayers," wrote Brother Lawrence, "and concentrate on being always in [God's] holy presence; I keep myself in [God's] presence by simple attentiveness and a loving gaze upon God."[6]

These exercises will invite you to practice some traditional forms of contemplative prayer—of turning your eyes to God in simplicity of faith and love. These forms may be unfamiliar to you but enter them with an openness that God may speak to you in new ways. Also you will receive the opportunity to assess where you are at this point in your journey of deepening prayer. Exercise 5 will serve as the basis of the sharing during this week's meeting.

EXERCISE 1: PRAYING WITH A PRAYER OF REPETITION

Read Philippians 2:12-13, where Paul identifies two parts of the spiritual life: our part (v. 12) and God's part (v. 13). Reflect on your role and God's role in your ongoing transformation in Christ. What is your awareness of the active presence of "God who is at work in you"? What is the quality of your cooperation with God "enabling you"?

Devote several minutes to praying the phrase "for it is God who is at work in you." Give your total attention to discerning the presence of God who is at work in you. Record expressions of your awareness in your journal.

EXERCISE 2: PRAYING WITH THE JESUS PRAYER

Read Luke 18:13, giving particular attention to the publican's prayer. Long ago, the publican's prayer became the basis for a contemplative prayer method called the Jesus Prayer, widely used in the Eastern

Orthodox Christian tradition. The most common form of the Jesus Prayer is "Lord Jesus Christ, Son of God, have mercy on me, a sinner." Sometimes persons abbreviate it to "Lord Jesus Christ, have mercy on me" or simply to "Lord Jesus, have mercy."

Spend some time praying the Jesus Prayer. Repeat it gently, letting the words focus your attention on God while expressing your need for grace. When you find your mind wandering, return to the prayer. Try developing an inner rhythm that suits you. For example, say the first half ("Lord Jesus Christ, Son of God") as you inhale and the second half ("have mercy on me, a sinner") as you exhale. Let the prayer move from the mind to the lips, until it gradually enters the heart. Allow it to foster an interior openness to God in the background of your daily activities.

EXERCISE 3: PRAYING WITH A VISUAL FOCUS

Read 2 Corinthians 3:18. In contemplative prayer, we are "seeing the glory" of God with "unveiled faces." Many Christians practice spiritual seeing by praying with a visual focus. Western Christians have commonly used the cross, a crucifix, or other works of art (including images in stained glass windows) to fix their inner eyes on Christ. Eastern Orthodox Christians commonly use icons (Greek for "image"), which are images of Christ and other saints that serve as windows onto spiritual reality.

Devote some time to "praying with your eyes," using a visual focus. Choose a cross, a favorite picture of Jesus, an icon, or a piece of art that draws you into the mystery of God. Inwardly express your desire to meet God. Gaze upon the visual focus without analyzing or evaluating what you see. Reach for God through your eyes, and let God reach for you through the "eyes" of the visual focus. Rather than seeking insights about God, seek to be seen and known by God. When distracted, calmly return your attention to the visual focus. After some minutes in this form of prayer, close your eyes, keeping your image in mind. Record your experience in your journal. As you move through the day, remember that you can also see the image of God in *people.*

EXERCISE 4: CENTERING PRAYER

What special words have power to lift your eyes to God and your heart to the Spirit? In centering prayer, we use a single word to focus on God and prepare ourselves for the gift of God's presence. The contemporary form of centering prayer, as presented by Thomas Keating, Basil Pennington, and others, is based on the teachings in a fourteenth-century classic called *The Cloud of Unknowing.*

Devote your daily exercise time to the practice of centering prayer. Choose a sacred word that represents your desire for God or God's yearning for you. A simple word is best, such as *love, God, Jesus, light, peace,* or *beloved*. Sit comfortably and close your eyes. Take several slow breaths to help you relax. Silently offer your sacred word to God as a sign of your desire for and consent to God's presence and action within. As you become aware of other thoughts, memories, feelings, or images, instead of fighting them, gently return to your sacred word. Remain in this state of rest and receptivity to God for approximately ten minutes. End with the Lord's Prayer or some other prayer. Remain quiet for a few more minutes. Write a few words in your journal about your experience.

EXERCISE 5: SCRIPTURAL CONTEMPLATION

Read Luke 10:38-42. The story of Martha and Mary illustrates the centrality of listening to God as a priority in the Christian life. During this final exercise, let the story of Martha and Mary guide you in discovering where you are in the journey of deepening prayer.

Reflect on the passage one verse at a time.

"[Jesus] entered a certain village, where a woman named Martha welcomed him into her home."

In what ways does Christ enter your awareness and life? How are you welcoming Christ in daily life, and what practices do you find most helpful?

"[Martha] had a sister named Mary, who sat at the Lord's feet and listened to what he was saying."

What obstacles did Mary have to overcome in deciding to leave the kitchen and sit at the Lord's feet? How have you grown and what challenges do you still face in learning to sit at the Lord's feet and listen?

"But Martha was distracted by her many tasks."

What continues to interrupt your presence to God in prayer or in daily life? Do as Martha did: Tell Jesus your trouble and what you think you need (v. 40). What is his response?

"There is need of only one thing."

What is the one thing you need in order to progress in prayer and love? What would Jesus say?

Now listen to the Lord. Imagine yourself sitting with Mary at the Lord's feet, listening to his teaching. Gaze into his face. What are you seeing in Jesus? What is Jesus seeing in you? What is he saying to you? After several minutes of loving attention to Jesus Christ, write notes in your journal from this time of communion.

Review your journal entries for the week in preparation for the group meeting.

Materials for Group Meetings

Developing Your Breath Prayer

The breath prayer is an ancient way of practicing the presence of God. It is a way to cultivate a posture of constant awareness and availability toward God.

Like prayers of repetition, breath prayers can be phrases from tradition, scripture, or hymnody. We repeat these phrases with our lips, carry them in our hearts, and whisper them under our breath.

The breath prayer is a way to act on your decision to be present to God who is always present to us. Practice your breath prayer at special times when you give God your undivided attention. Continue to say your breath prayer under your breath; let it become a habit of the heart.

Spend a few minutes now in developing and praying your breath prayer. Write it down as a reminder to keep with your journal.

Ron DelBene (pronounced like bane), a contemporary author of books on the spiritual life, has written extensively on creating and using personal breath prayers. The following steps are taken from his book *The Breath of Life: A Workbook*.

STEP ONE
Sit in a comfortable position. Close your eyes and remind yourself that God loves you and that you are in God's loving presence. Recall a passage of scripture that puts you in a prayerful frame of mind. Consider "The Lord is my shepherd" (Ps. 23:1) or "Be still, and know that I am God" (Ps. 46:10).

STEP TWO
With your eyes still closed, imagine that God is calling you by name. Hear God asking you: "(*Your name*), what do you want?"

MANTRA

STEP THREE

Answer God with whatever comes directly from your heart. Your answer might be a single word, such as *peace* or *love* or *forgiveness*. Your answer could instead be a phrase or brief sentence, such as "I want to feel your forgiveness" or "I want to know your love."

Because the prayer is personal, it naturally rises out of our present concerns.... Your response to God's question "What do you want?" becomes the heart of your prayer.

STEP FOUR

Choose your favorite name or image for God. Choices commonly made include God, Jesus, Creator, Teacher, Light, Lord, Spirit, Shepherd.

STEP FIVE

Combine your name for God with your answer to God's question "What do you want?" You then have your prayer. For example:

What I Want	Name I Call God	Possible Prayer
Peace	God	Let me know your peace, O God.
Love	Jesus	Jesus, let me feel your love.
Rest	Shepherd	My Shepherd, let me rest in thee.
Guidance	Eternal Light	Eternal Light, guide me in your way.

What do you do if several ideas occur? Write down the various possibilities and then eliminate and/or combine ideas until you have focused your prayer. You may want many things, but it is possible to narrow wants to those most basic to your well-being. Thus, the question to ask yourself is: *What do I want that will make me feel most whole?* As you achieve a greater feeling of wholeness, serenity will flow into the many areas of your life.

When you have gotten to the heart of your deep yearning, search for words that give it expression. Then work with the words until you have a prayer of six to eight syllables that flows smoothly when spoken aloud or expressed as a heart thought. A prayer of six to eight syllables has a natural rhythm. Anything longer or shorter usually does not flow easily when said repeatedly. Some prayers are more rhythmic when you place God's name at the beginning; other prayers flow better with it at the end.

Ron DelBene, *The Breath of Life: A Workbook* (Nashville, Tenn.: The Upper Room, 1996), 12–13. Used by permission of Upper Room Books.

An Annotated Resource List from Upper Room Ministries

*T*he following books relate to and expand on the subject matter of this third volume of *Companions in Christ*. As you read and share with your small group, you may find some material that particularly challenges or helps you. If you wish to pursue individual reading on your own or if your small group wishes to follow up with additional resources, this list may be useful. The Upper Room is the publisher of all of the books listed, and the number in parentheses is the order number.

1. *Creating a Life with God: The Call of Ancient Prayer Practices* (#9855) by Daniel Wolpert. This book introduces you to twelve prayer practices that invite you to solitude and silence, to use your mind and imagination, to use your body and your creativity, and to connect with nature and community.

2. *Dimensions of Prayer: Cultivating a Relationship with God* (#971) by Douglas V. Steere is a classic on prayer, first published in 1962 and revised in this new edition published in 1997. Steere, in his warm and engaging style, writes about the basic issues of prayer—why we pray, what prayer is, how to pray, what prayer does to us and to our activity in the world. Tilden Edwards says that reading this book is like sitting at the feet of one the wisest spiritual leaders of the twentieth century and hearing what are the important things he has learned about prayer over a lifetime.

3. *Teach Me to Pray* (#125) by W. E. Sangster is another classic on prayer that focuses on the importance of prayer in the life of a Christian and on ways to develop a strong and intimate prayer life with God. Sangster wrote a section of this book on practical questions about prayer, a section on how to form prayer groups, and a section on how we learn to "live in Christ." This book has been recently revised and updated.

4. *Traveling the Prayer Paths of Jesus* (#9857) by John Indermark. "The discipline of prayer forms the cornerstone of Christian spirituality." Join Jesus in places of prayer and learn

from the daily readings that examine Jesus' prayers in six different settings: out of solitude, by the roadside, on the mountainside, in the upper room, at the garden, upon the cross.

5. *The Workbook of Living Prayer* (#718) by Maxie Dunnam is a six-week study on prayer. It includes material for daily readings and prayers with reflection suggestions. The tremendous popularity and widespread use of this workbook demonstrate its effectiveness in a variety of settings and attest to the essential, time-tested nature of the teachings it contains about prayer. The author gives special attention to what we learn from Christ about the life of prayer.

6. *Responding to God* (#783) by Martha Graybeal Rowlett is a resource that helps us understand prayer as a response to God's grace in our lives. This book and accompanying leader's guide contain a suggested model for daily prayer and material for ten weeks of study on the various facets of prayer. It includes chapters on our understanding of God, the forms of prayer, the difference prayer makes in the life of the believer, and why some prayers go unanswered. The leader's guide (#926) also offers suggestions on using the book for different time frames, such as six weeks, twelve weeks, or a weekend retreat.

7. *Praying in the Wesleyan Spirit: 52 Prayers for Today* (#950) by Paul Chilcote. By converting Wesley's sermons into prayers, Dr. Chilcote has faithfully rendered both the substance and the intent of john Wesley's proclamation—a means of divine encounter for nothing less than the regeneration of the lost, the reformation of society, and the renewal of the church.

Continue your exploration of deepening your prayer by using *Companions in Christ: The Way of Forgiveness* with your small group.

The Way of Forgiveness
By Marjorie J. Thompson and Stephen D. Bryant
Participant's Book (0-8358-0980-3)
Leader's Guide (0-8358-0981-1)

The Way of Forgiveness uses scripture to guide participants through a nine-week exploration of the forgiven and forgiving life. Weekly topics in this challenging and rewarding study include Releasing Our Shame and Guilt, Facing Our Anger, Transforming Anger, Receiving God's Forgiveness, Forgiving Others, and Seeking Reconciliation.

Notes

Week 1   Prayer and the Character of God

1. Marjorie J. Thompson, *Soul Feast*, (Louisville, Ky.: Westminster John Knox Press, 2005), 33.
2. Augustine, *Confessions* 10. 27. 38, trans. J. G. Pilkington, Nicene and Post-Nicene Fathers, First Series, vol. 1 (1886; reprint, Peabody, Mass.: Hendrickson Publishers, 1994), 152–53. Adapted by Keith Beasley-Topliffe.

Week 2   Dealing with Impediments to Prayer

1. Jean-Pierre de Caussade, *Abandonment to Divine Providence*, trans. John Beevers (New York: Image Books, 1975), 72.
2. Douglas V. Steere, *Dimensions of Prayer* (Nashville, Tenn.: Upper Room Books, 1997), xx.

Week 3   Prayers of Petition and Intercession

1. Steere, *Dimensions of Prayer*, 69.
2. Maria Boulding, *The Coming of God* (Collegeville, Minn.: The Liturgical Press, 1982), 7–8.

Week 4   Praying As We Are

1. Harvey D. Egan, "Negative Way," in *The New Dictionary of Catholic Spirituality* (Collegeville, Minn.: The Liturgical Press, 1993), 700.
2. James Finley, as quoted by Allan H. Sager, *Gospel-Centered Spirituality* (Minneapolis, Minn.: Augsburg Fortress, 1990), 37.
3. Urban T. Holmes III, *A History of Christian Spirituality: An Analytical Introduction* (New York: Seabury, 1980), 4–5.
4. For a more detailed description of the four types, see Corinne Ware, *Discover Your Spiritual Type* (Bethesda, Md.: The Alban Institute, 1995).
5. Ibid., 43.
6. Ibid., 44–45.
7. Karl Rahner, *Encounters with Silence*, trans. James M. Demske (Westminster, Md.: The Newman Press, 1960), 15–16.
8. Dom Chapman, as quoted in Richard Foster's book *Prayer: Finding the Heart's True Home* (San Francisco: HarperSanFrancisco, 1992), 7.

Week 5   Psalms, the Prayer Book of the Bible

1. Thomas R. Hawkins, *The Unsuspected Power of the Psalms* (Nashville, Tenn.: The Upper Room, 1985), 37.

Week 6   Exploring Contemplative Prayer

1. William H. Shannon, "Contemplation, Contemplative Prayer," in *The New Dictionary of Catholic Spirituality*, 209.
2. Augustine, *Confessions* 1.1, ed. Keith Beasley-Topliffe, Upper Room Spiritual Classics, Series 1 (Nashville, Tenn.: Upper Room Books, 1997), 12.
3. Teresa of Avila, *The Interior Castle* in *The Collected Works of St. Teresa of Avila*, vol. 2, trans. Kieran Kavanaugh and Otilio Rodriguez (Washington, D.C.: Institute of Carmelite Studies, 1980), 283.

Notes

4. Teresa of Avila, *The Book of Her Life* in *The Collected Works of St. Teresa of Avila*, vol. 1, trans. Kieran Kavanaugh and Otilio Rodriguez (Washington, D.C.: Institute of Carmelite Studies, 1976), 80.
5. Teresa of Avila, *The Interior Castle*, 430.
6. Brother Lawrence of the Resurrection, *The Practice of the Presence of God*, trans. John J. Delaney (New York: Image Books, 1977), 68.

Sources and Authors of Margin Quotations

Week 1   Prayer and the Character of God
Martha Graybeal Rowlett, *Responding to God* (Nashville, Tenn.: Upper Room Books, 1996), 29.

Margaret Guenther, *The Practice of Prayer* (Cambridge, Mass.: Cowley Publications, 1998), 16.

George MacDonald, *The Diary of an Old Soul* (London: George Allen & Unwin, 1905), 17.

Boulding, *The Coming of God*, 20.

Douglas V. Steere, *Dimensions of Prayer* (Nashville, Tenn.: Upper Room Books, 1997), 12.

Week 2   Dealing with Impediments to Prayer
John Killinger, *Beginning Prayer* (Nashville, Tenn.: Upper Room Books, 1993), 16.

Teresa of Avila, *The Interior Castle,* trans. Kieran Kavanaugh and Otilio Rodriguez (New York: Paulist Press, 1979) 53.

John Calvin, "Of Prayer" in *Institutes of the Christian Religion*, trans. Henry Beveridge (27 May 1999) <http://www.ccel.org/c/calvin/prayer/prayer.html> (14 July 2000), sec. 50.

Thomas R. Kelly, *A Testament of Devotion* (New York: Harper & Row, 1941), 60.

Week 3   Prayers of Petition and Intercession
Emilie Griffin, *Clinging: The Experience of Prayer* (New York: McCracken Press, 1994), 5.

Henri J. M. Nouwen, *The Genesee Diary* (New York: Image Books, 1989), 145.

Toyohiko Kagawa, *Meditations on the Cross* as cited in *Living Out Christ's Love: Selected Writings of Toyohiko Kagawa*, ed. Keith Beasley-Topliffe (Nashville, Tenn.: Upper Room Books, 1998), 57.

William Law, *A Serious Call to a Devout and Holy Life* (Philadelphia: The Westminster Press, 1948), 308.

Week 4   Praying As We Are
Kenneth Leech, *True Prayer* (San Francisco: Harper & Row, 1980), 3.

Timothy Jones, *The Art of Prayer* (New York: Ballantine Books, 1997), 122.

Catherine de Hueck Doherty, *Soul of My Soul* (Notre Dame, Ind.: Ave Maria Press, 1985), 113.

Week 5   Psalms, the Prayer Book of the Bible
Walter Brueggemann, *Praying the Psalms* (Winona, Minn.: Saint Mary's Press, 1982), 17.

Kathleen Norris, *The Psalms,* (New York: Riverhead Books, 1997), viii.

Larry R. Kalajainen, *Psalms for the Journey* (Nashville, Tenn.: Upper Room Books, 1996), 10.

Week 6   Exploring Contemplative Prayer
Thomas Merton, *Contemplative Prayer* (Garden City, N.Y.: Image Books, 1971), 89.

Tilden H. Edwards, "Living the Day from the Heart," from *The Weavings Reader* (Nashville, Tenn.: Upper Room Books, 1993), 58.

Mother Teresa, *A Life for God: The Mother Teresa Treasury*, comp. LaVonne Neff (London: Fount, 1997), 17–18.

Henri J. M. Nouwen, *Making All Things New* (San Francisco: Harper & Row, 1981), 57.

COMPANION SONG
Piano Accompaniment Score

Lyrics by Marjorie Thompson   Music by Dean McIntyre

Optional cut for short version: omit measures 19-34.

Companions in Christ
Part 3 Author

Adele J. Gonzalez is the founder and president of Get-With-It, LLC an organization committed to human and spiritual growth through the fostering of healthy relationships with self, others, the world, and God. She has been involved in Christian formation, spiritual guidance, and retreat ministry for over 35 years in the Roman Catholic Church. Adele is a national speaker and has recently published the books *Anger: a Positive Energy* and *The Depth and Richness of the Scriptures.* She is a lay associate of the Sisters of St. Francis, Stella Niagara, New York.

Journal